What people are sa

The Art of You

Intelligently-written and timely, this book is filled with practical psycho-spiritual techniques and teachings, many of them grounded in the powerful roots of ancient wisdom traditions. Vanessa's experience, expertise and artistic nature shine through as she thoughtfully guides and enables women to consciously and creatively walk their own path of authenticity and power.

Christa Mackinnon, Psychologist, Therapist, Shamanic Teacher and Hay House Author *Shamanism (basics)*, *Shamanism and Spirituality in Therapeutic Practice*

Compelling and enchanting this book is an advocate of wild authenticity and vital beauty. Vanessa's intuitive wisdom and enlightening insights act as creative catalysts for us all. You are left inspired to create an authentic and 'artful' life.

Jamie Catto, artist (Faithless), author *Insanely Gifted*

This is a Hero's / Heroine's Journey. This is an archetypal story whose resonances touch us all – starting life on one path, the crisis moment, the rebirth, and the lifting of the veil to reveal a fuller, richer, more fulfilling life. Vanessa walks her talk and has a beautiful toolkit to help others do the same.

Joe Hoare, coach, author *Awakening the Laughing Buddha Within*

This book is a powerful reminder, in a busy and complicated world, of carving time and space for self and for reflection. It invites women to look at themselves and the world differently, through new lenses and to recognise the creative energy of womanhood.

Professor Debra Myhill, Pro-Vice-Chancellor, College of Social Sciences and International Studies, University of Exeter

The Art of You is wonderfully playful and optimistic! Vanessa Tucker explains how to find and connect with our inner "co-creator" by unmaking entrenched habits and overcoming fears that stand in the way of a truly rewarding and responsive life. *The Art of You* demonstrates that learning to observe, listen to and trust our intuitions, other people and the world around us is vital to release creativity and nurture positive power.

Professor Frances Babbage, author *Re-Visioning Myth: Modern and Contemporary Drama by Women* and *Augusto Boal*

The Art of You

A Guide to Shaping Your Unique
Place in the Beautiful Mosaic of Life

The Art of You

A Guide to Shaping Your Unique
Place in the Beautiful Mosaic of Life

Vanessa Tucker

BOOKS
Winchester, UK
Washington, USA

JOHN HUNT PUBLISHING

First published by O-Books, 2019
O-Books is an imprint of John Hunt Publishing Ltd., 3 East St., Alresford,
Hampshire SO24 9EE, UK
office@jhpbooks.net
www.johnhuntpublishing.com
www.o-books.com

For distributor details and how to order please visit the 'Ordering' section on our website.

Text copyright: Vanessa Tucker 2018
Cover design & Illustrations copyright: Stephanie Ayres Illustration

ISBN: 978 1 78904 107 1
978 1 78904 108 8 (ebook)
Library of Congress Control Number: 2018941703

A CIP catalogue record for this book is available from the British Library.

Design: Stuart Davies

UK: Printed and bound by CPI Group (UK) Ltd, Croydon, CR0 4YY
US: Printed and bound by Thomson-Shore, 7300 West Joy Road, Dexter, MI 48130

We operate a distinctive and ethical publishing philosophy in
all areas of our business, from our global network of authors to
production and worldwide distribution.

Contents

Dedicated To Maisie The Stargazer
may you shine brightly

Prologue

How do we uncover a greater story to live? Let's begin by painting a picture...

The Advertisement

An aspiring actress responded to this casting call:

Wanted: A fictional victim

Gender: Female

Age: Open to all

Acting ability needed to portray a princess who needs saving, tries hard but remains insignificant, is self-doubting, self-loathing, unlovable and overly responsible for the needs of others.

Required attributes:

Secretly believes she is too fat, too ugly, too stupid, too tired, too clumsy, too emotional, too sensitive, too much, not good enough and skilled at disregarding her needs.

An undeserving, rejected demeanour is vital. Trauma is an asset, but not essential. Must be able to commit to denial, have something to hide, be able to please and have good improvisation skills. Crown provided.

Years later she was sick to death of squeezing herself into this restricting role; it had grown excruciatingly painful, so much so that she opened her mouth and unleashed a hankering howl. Her blinkers collapsed on the floor and the audience shuddered. Sure that there was more to life than this, she grabbed her coat and leapt off the stage into the darkness.

Her crown had vanished and she realised there was no longer any need to bear the weight of the heavy sack full of trauma that she had carried with her everywhere. She carefully placed the sack on the muddy soil next to her. She removed her coat of tales, exquisitely woven and heavily embroidered with outdated, moth-ridden stories, and suddenly she was naked, vulnerable and cold.

There was nothing to do but lie down in her puddle of pain and gaze at the stars.

A chill had captured the air and in search of warmth she reached for the sack and released the brittle string. Out tumbled her Tales of the Unexpected, untold and grim. She sat for a moment in hesitation, but curiosity got the better of her. As she devoured each page, her perception expanded and her power illuminated. She closed the book and saw a great truth, she saw light, she saw possibility, she saw beauty, she was with the stars, she was one of them. She thanked herself for leaving that limiting stage; her next discovery was how to answer her creative calling and play her starring role here on earth...

(If you'd like to read her Tales of the Unexpected you'll find them on page 221.)

Director's Notes

The PIE root word of art is 'ar' – meaning 'join together'. It's my intention that this is exactly what this book will do for you. It will join you with your unexpressed parts, your place and purpose here on earth, and your cosmic powers. You will be able to see your unique beauty and express it in the world.

The artist must find her own way, and this book does not tell you what you must or must not do, rather I hope you will use it as a guide to explore your space and uncover new worlds. It offers you practical and creative ways to deal with life's challenges and paves the way for you to find and express your purpose in the world.

This book guides you in a linear fashion, each chapter building on the knowledge of the previous one, but by all means break the rules, dip in, and explore it as you feel inspired to do.

Each chapter explores a different way of looking at yourself and your place in the world. I hope its essence inspires, provokes, encourages and supports you, as it has me.

Part One, The Bigger Picture: Feeding Your Roots, lays the foundation for all the creative work you are about to do. It rewilds you; plugs you back into the whole, plumps up your roots of existence and gives you the tools to 'untame' your beautiful nature.

Firstly, you will awaken your Life Artist – the wise woman within, and learn how to see through her eyes. You will be able to build a vision of yourself that you love and that brings joy to others. Next, you will revive the three cosmic powers that sustain your wholeness, power and growth: Nature feeds your belonging, energy feeds your quality of life, and beauty feeds your soul. United they act as the cement that holds your part of the cosmic mosaic in place. They will keep you aligned, whilst deepening your natural spiritual connection.

With your Life Artist at the ready, and your cosmic powers flowing freely, you have the perfect foundation to begin shaping yourself as a work of art.

Part Two, The Living Bridges: Shaping Your Roots, offers you insight and access into different realities and other ways of seeing. Step onto the bridges and explore worlds rich in possibility, support and discovery. Once you have trodden these paths, you will feel empowered, connected, and able to shape your life to follow your purpose. You will know how to work alongside your co-creator and follow your guidance to show up and play your part.

Art gives life shape and this is exactly what the living bridges will do for you. You can use them to shape your life producing a beautiful soul-centred way of being. The more you use them, the stronger they, and you, will become.

This isn't a quick fix book, although once you start working with it, you'll observe that your life shifts as rapidly as your perception. Rather it acts as a reminder of the constant choice available to you, a way of seeing. It distils the thirty years' experience, knowledge and learning from my personal, spiritual, and professional work and wraps them up as practical tools you can use to express the beauty that is you.

You can look at yourself as an unfolding work of art, beautiful in the moment and growing as a masterpiece every day. This book is an invitation for you to shine brightly, to fill your life with beauty, meaning and purpose.

Chapter 1

Setting the Scene

Are You Ready To Answer Your Creative Calling?

Can you hear its haunting howl?

Just like a restless lone wolf, an unanswered creative call has a tendency to leave you feeling stuck and divided, with no sense of belonging; dulling your vision with shadows of self-doubt and inadequacy. Simply put – it shrinks your life and starves your soul, until you tend to it.

You are probably reading this book because deep inside your heart you know. You know there is more to life; you know life is precious and beautiful; you know you matter. But right now, you are not seeing it. Perhaps you've recently experienced a life-changing shake-up, like a divorce or illness, and you are struggling to find your next step. Maybe you are disenchanted with the work you do or the company you keep. Or maybe it's something you can't quite put your finger on. Are you tired of it all? Has life lost its beauty?

You have a choice to how you view this time in your life. All of the above are signs that life is offering you an opportunity to take notice of your soul's longing and remember your beauty, uniqueness and significance.

Trust Your Stirring Soul

You're not alone, many of us – sisters, mothers and grandmothers – are feeling and answering this creative call to rise up and shine. If you trust your stirring soul, you'll see it is guiding you to carve out your path to wholeness. There is much more to life, and to you. And you don't have to be 'Good at art' to discover it.

This book will guide you through a creative process to reconnect you with your power and to cultivate your unique presence and expression. You will feel supported to answer your creative calling and share your beauty with the world.

How Do You Get Started?

The simple answer is: You harness your gift of vision and you get creative!

You see yourself as an ever-unfolding work of art, beautiful in the moment and growing as a masterpiece every day. When you look at how you are creating life and how life is creating you, you empower your choices – your perception expands, you can spot your potential, and your sense of purpose and belonging becomes firmly rooted in all you do.

Why Art?

Each piece of art carries a great story and a story of greatness. It asks something of the world with its message and brings truth to life with beauty and question. You too can access your true nature and unveil your story of greatness. *The Art of You* invites you to look, to see, to ask these reality-busting questions:

- What is my truth?
- What is my message?
- What is my purpose?
- What are the stories I'm carrying?
- What is my great story?

And it offers you creative ways to discover the answers.

But I'm Not Creative!

Countless times I've heard my clients and students say: "But I'm not creative." "It's not really me; my sister's the arty one." This fear of creativity is one of the reasons I decided to write *The*

Art of You – I want to help you to see that you are continuously creating; you are both a walking masterpiece and a creative artist. You create with every breath you take, and just like breathing, you cannot stop it. Our brains are wired to create. If you've ever decorated your home, you've been creative; if you've cooked a meal, run out of ingredients, and then decided to throw in the next best thing, you've been creative. If you've been making up excuses for your partner's behaviour all these years or escaped from an online date that wasn't quite as you imagined, you've been creative! You've experimented and played – that's creativity in action and the more you use your creative muscle, the easier it becomes, and the better you get at it.

You see, the "I'm not creative" barrier has little to do with ability and everything to do with perception and belief. It's a disempowering way of looking at yourself that keeps you small – like wearing a set of horse's blinkers – your vision is limited and your awareness is restricted. In my experience, working with both adults and children, there are two main reasons why people see themselves in this way.

1. They overthink the outcome: Standing at the bottom of the mountain the task at hand grows too big and overwhelming. They compare themselves with all the flags already flying at the top, then they give up and get a cup of tea.

2. They believe they have nothing original to contribute and feel that they will fail. They avoid failure at all costs by not starting; they go and get another cup of tea.

A lot of tea drinking and hanging around happens while waiting for the creative kettle to boil!

There is another way...

Develop Your Empowering Gaze

As you work throughout the book you will encounter five liberating ways of seeing that will support you to develop your empowering gaze. These practical concepts – the Star-Studded Cosmic Mosaic, Alchemy Moments, the Life Artist, the three Cosmic Powers, and the Living Bridges – are all designed to shift and expand your perception – to finally remove the blinkers keeping you small.

You will be free to adopt the eagle's viewpoint – one of flexibility, wonder, and clarity. The eagle's eye is remarkable; it has a vast 340-degree visual field, while also acting as a telephoto lens, giving it extra magnification for hunting prey. Eagles also see colours more vividly than we do and can discriminate between a larger variety of shades.

You can develop this powerful gaze when you see yourself as both the artist and the art. Life looks beautiful from this position, and you have the capacity to manifest the impossible, the invisible, and the unknown. You can spot your story of greatness, zoom in on your unique message, and capture your truth.

Creating my life from the eagle's viewpoint of both art and artist has helped me to transcend limits, transform trauma, discover gifts and share them with the world. It has helped me to see my true beauty.

It wasn't always this way for me. Even though I classed myself as a creative person, with a background in the arts, I'd never applied the eagle eye to myself or my personal life until I experienced an awakening back in 2004. My life was smashed to bits in one blow, and I fell off my stage with a huge thud. I won't lie – it hurt like hell, but it was the best thing that could have happened to me. I unleashed my wise woman; became a Life Artist and met my Creatrix. Your Creatrix will show you your gifts, dreams and talents, ones you may never have imagined – like writing a book for example! Or running your own business.

You will feel a calling to keep growing, and to become familiar with change, which is challenging. Nobody likes change. But here's the thing – when you understand fully that you are in a constant state of artistic expression, and that you are driving it forward, you become liberated, empowered and have compassion for yourself. And you develop a healthy balanced relationship with change.

When those tough times arrive, and they will, remember you are part of nature, think of yourself as a flower, you are supposed to be beautiful, extraordinary and significant and you're here on the planet to express it as only you can. Keep blooming, nurture new buds, and focus on your place in the bigger picture, stay aligned and you'll keep growing into 'all that you can be' by living a fulfilling and beautiful existence.

The Star-Studded Mosaic

Behind the cotton wool of daily reality is a hidden pattern. We – I mean all human beings – are connected with this. The whole world is a work of art and we are parts of the work of art.
– Virginia Woolf

While I was writing this book, I went to Barcelona and visited the artist Gaudi's Parc Guell. The Spanish architect and artist's work was heavily inspired by nature, and he coated much of his work in exquisite mosaics. I was strolling through this whimsical tribute to nature's beauty, trying to conjure up a simple metaphor for our connection with the cosmos and our role in nature. And then, voila, I sat on it! My bottom was cradled by the Serpentine bench made entirely from mosaics, each piece a glorious work of art in its own right. Both the individual pieces and complete mosaic pattern exist as a harmonious whole and gives great pleasure to all who look or sit on it!

This is exactly what we are – individual pieces of art belonging to one beautiful, star-studded, cosmic mosaic, except ours is an expanding pattern. Each one of us has a purpose, an individual destiny of beauty to fulfil. We each contain a unique, meaningful message. The whole works through us, and we shape the whole. Your presence contributes to the bigger picture and therefore what you do matters.

You only need glimpse this evening's transcendent sunset to be reminded that you exist in a work of art. And likewise, we only need to be shown life's tragedies, to know that what we do affects the whole picture. The trouble is that most of the time we don't look, and we don't include ourselves as part of the picture.

Growing with the expanding cosmic pattern is important. When we resist growing, we move out of alignment, life gets tough and sometimes, just like the pieces of the mosaic, we need to break to fit back in and reshape our reality to see our creative calling. I call these times life's Alchemy Moments.

Alchemy Moments

Alchemy Moments are powerful life transformations that act as catalysts. They come along when we have resisted our creative call for too long, offering us opportunities to put down new roots and grow, uncovering our gold to become more than we ever thought possible.

My Alchemy Moment No. 1

The Persistent Soul

My career journey started when I was sixteen, and I walked into the grey, stale-smelling careers office at school. The lonely-looking spinster peeked over her glasses and asked, with a tone of regret: "What do you want to do with your life."

"It's my dream to be an actress," I said. I had been acting and singing since I was 12 years old. I loved it – it set me free.

The careers officer sighed. "Ninety per cent of actors are out of work all the time," she said. "What proper job would you like to do?"

I chose hairdressing and worked as a stylist for more than a decade. It was here I became fascinated with our fundamental relationship to art and beauty.

I then had what I now call an "Alchemy Moment". The reason I call them Alchemy 'Moments' is because they feel as though you are stuck in a never-ending moment of time. Yet, they are a deeply transformative process: Firstly, they pierce through your bubble of reality and deflate it. Then they put cracks in the earth you stand upon, forcing you to see the stagnant waters you are wading through, and finally, they invite you to create new pathways of alignment, which bring fresh flowing life into your world. This is often painful as we resist the process of leaving behind what is not wanted in our lives – especially hard when we believe we need it!

For a long while, I had resisted what I knew deep down in my soul wasn't right. Again and again I had chosen to ignore my intuitive voice because I was scared to face my stagnant life. At 24 my denial had left me rejected, humiliated and devastated. I discovered my fiancé was cheating again and had also been lying about making the mortgage payments. I cancelled the wedding arrangements, cleared my home for the repossession and had nothing more to lose.

I found myself back in my parents' home, and life seemed dark and empty. It was in this exquisite darkness that I answered my soul's calling from all those years before – I decided to follow my heart and become an actress. I also made a vow to take responsibility for myself – I needed to earn enough money to support myself so I never had to rely on a man again.

I worked relentlessly – during the daytime I squeezed in as many clients as possible to save money for university, and in the evenings, I studied for an access course to gain the qualifications I needed to be offered a place. What seemed like an unreachable dream at the time provided me with a degree in Drama, English and Psychology and a performance career.

Answering your soul's calling will lead you to grow in the most unexpected places...

It was a usual bleak and rainy evening as the prison walls closed in on me. With my heart beating madly I stayed close to the guard as he twisted an eternity of keys. His echoing footprints and the stench of institution led me to the performance room. I'd been writing a thesis on the therapeutic potential of drama in prisons and had been working with the inmates on a production of Snow White *for a couple of months now; this was our opening night. Over the course of my research, I had conducted case studies and interviews exploring how theatre opened up a healing space that was both cathartic and transformative for all who entered it. In the act of being observed and observing magic happened – limitation shifted, potential was seen, and people were united.*

I entered the stage in front of one of the toughest and most unforgiving audiences – in my experience inmates are second only to a class of schoolchildren! The performers were nervous and had received threats that some of the other inmates would intentionally wreck the show. It was tense, to say the least.

After a while, the nerves settled, and the performance was in full swing. I then had a surreal out of body experience. I was looking down on myself. I watched myself as a singing dwarf, with an audience of inmates, guards, and performers. One by one everyone in the room stood up, and at the top of their voices, we were united in singing Monty Python's Always Look on the Bright Side of Life. *We became one, if only for a moment, and I was hooked on the transformational power of the arts.*

Although I had a fantastic time performing with theatre companies, my soul, research and experiences naturally guided me towards the therapeutic and healing potential of drama. I continued to learn and research; spending the next 15 years in education as a teacher of drama and performing arts, but waiting in the wings was another heart-wrenching Alchemy Moment.

Alchemy Moment No. 2

Marriage, Death & Rebirth

This second 'moment' happened in 2003 and brought me an awakening – or reawakening. In a fast and furious process, I lost everything that was important to me: my new marriage, my amazing husband and my home. At the end of this dark and painful separation, I had also lost myself. I had evaporated.

At the time, I didn't understand I was in the process of alchemy that would turn my life golden. That's the most painful thing, the lack of realisation that something positive and transformational is happening. Now I know it's a process, an opportunity, a way of keeping in alignment with the greater pattern.

It was during this time that I listened to my soul and took action. I answered the question that kept popping into my head: "What would you do if you only had six months to live?" I leapt into the unknown, took a sabbatical and went travelling for a year. I drank the elixir, discovered the magic of life and expressed my beauty. My faith in humanity and spiritual connection to something greater than myself was restored – I had uncovered a greater story to live. (You can read the full story of this enlightening time in the following chapter.)

When I arrived home, I unpacked eternal knowingness, a vision of myself I loved, and a wealth of psychic and healing gifts.

I had a driven purpose and hungered for spiritual growth; I became a reiki master, crystal healer, shamanic practitioner, hypnotherapist and NLP practitioner while continuing to work part-time as a drama teacher. I established my healing business, developed Alchemy Medicine – my integrated healing system – and expanded my skills. And I kept a vow that I made to myself that I would continue to travel solo every year to India to revive and expand my energy.

Alchemy Moment No. 3

Listen, Act & Create

My third Alchemy Moment happened six years later. It was very different from the first two. This time, I co-created with Spirit, I was a Life Artist. There was no excruciating pain, only some fear and self-doubt.

The previous few years had become hard to manage. Running a business alongside working in education was breaking me. My heart, body, mind and soul had become weary. I was evaporating, again. I knew this depletion of energy well, the dull drudgery and feeling stuck in my tightly-structured existence were shrinking me. I was trying to fill the void of my soul's joy with destructive habits, material things, and safety. Life was asking me, once again, to follow my dreams. So, I started a revolution from my bed! John Lennon would be proud of me.

One Sunday morning I sat in bed with my partner. Together we decided to make a dream sheet of what we wanted from our lives. I drew a heart and we began writing. I felt an inner flame rise as I wrote the words "I'd love to spend six months in India and six months in the UK. I want to develop and share my healing work and be financially supported by it. I want to keep travelling and growing."

A week later I walked into work, supported by Jill Scott singing, "I'm living my life like it's golden," through my headphones. I took a huge breath and boldly placed a letter of resignation on the desk of the headmaster's PA. Fifteen years in education ended and my identity and financial security were wiped away with that one action. In a world of economic depression, I felt great! This was heart in action; I felt my soul dance. I smiled, flicked my hair, held my head high and Walk Your Talk Retreats, Courses & Workshops was born.

Taking this risk helped me to uncover my gifts and help others. Initially, I felt guided to create retreats for people experiencing

Alchemy Moments who required healing and support. Over the years this has extended into a variety of spiritual workshops, training and programmes, and as well as an established healing practice, I now provide training in my Alchemy Medicine healing system. This is Walk Your Talk Retreats' seventh year. They take place in India in a breathtaking location by the ocean and in various places in the UK. Being a success right from the start, the retreats and workshops continue to grow and expand, supporting many in uncovering their true nature, discovering their potential and creating lives they love, while giving me a life that is fulfilling, exciting and heart-centred.

Your Co-Creator Is Your 'Other Half'

All the world may be a stage, but you are not "merely" the player resigned to acting out your given roles and circumstances. You are the pattern-cutter, the storyteller, the director, the designer, the painter, the sculptor. You are a powerful co-creator; a Life Artist working in harmony with the divine.

You will notice that I have mentioned that you are co-creating – that is not creating alone. You may be wondering what I mean by that. There is something beautiful working behind the scenes; in our lives, here on earth, and beyond. Something greater than us and we are part of it.

This mysterious and intelligent force is sacred, yet in everyday life, we often forget its presence. It's known as God, the Great Spirit, the Divine, the Universe, the Tao, the Whole, Source, depending on different belief systems. Throughout the book, I will mostly use the term Divine or Great Spirit. You can choose to name it as you wish.

What is important is to communicate with your co-creator and bring this sacred mystery into your beautiful creations. When you collaborate intimately with your co-creator, they become your 'other half', making you whole. You will be guided towards the space that contains your potential and your purpose in life, and shown how you fit into the expanding mosaic of life. You will know that you matter and that the whole is working through you.

See Yourself as a Work of Art

What does it mean to see yourself as a work of art?

As you will discover, a piece of art expresses something beautiful or meaningful; it holds and translates truth, unveiling life's mysteries. It's the expression of the artist's soul, the unexplored parts, helping the artist to contribute something sacred within themselves to the world around them.

Art captures human consciousness and reveals for all to see.

Here's a playful exercise to get started:

First, read this sentence:

"Art makes other worlds visible and shows us a new possible reality. It captures possibility and potential showing us other ways of being. Art has meaning and beauty. Art is not about perfection and can be uncomfortable, challenging and downright dirty at times. It challenges, provokes and stands for itself."

Now I'm going to replace the word "art" with my name and repeat that sentence:

"Vanessa... makes other worlds visible and shows us a new possible reality, she expresses truth, connects us with our soul, captures possibility and potential, showing us other ways of being. Vanessa has meaning and beauty. Vanessa is not about perfection and can be uncomfortable, challenging and downright dirty at times. She challenges, provokes and stands for herself."

Next, try it with your name.

How does that feel? Is it challenging? Empowering? Uncomfortable? Does it set too high a precedent for you? Do you glimpse a truth about your beautiful role in the bigger scheme of things?

Your masterpiece can bring fresh hope to the world. This empowering position is often excruciatingly uncomfortable to hold at first, mainly due to feelings of unworthiness – that doubt of "Who am I to raise myself up?" Playing small is a habit that infects and pollutes everything around you. It's cancerous, it eats away at your growth, joy and hope, it stunts your life, and it stops you carrying out your specific role of beauty in the great cosmic mosaic. In my experience, it's also as difficult a habit to break as smoking, and that's where your Life Artist comes in.

Becoming a Life Artist will help you release this habit. You can break down your personal limitations, awaken your natural powers and rise up to be seen in all your exquisite beauty.

Let's get started...

Part I

The Bigger Picture: Feeding Your Roots

Chapter 2

Becoming a Life Artist

Let's paint a picture....

The Flower That Never Was

Marigold the flower believed that if she opened up her petals she might be trampled upon by big boots or blown away to some strange land. This fear made her hide inside her comfortable, protective pod for ever. She never experienced herself in bloom. She never shared her gift of blossom with the world, so she never brought anyone any joy. She never fulfilled her purpose and she never knew her true beauty. She was, however, safe. But then again, she never was...

Living without the beauty of your true nature is like the Earth without the Sun. It is your Life Artist who holds the creative key to set your Marigold free. She can make your garden grow and help you to see a reflection of yourself that you love. But first you need to find her.

How My Life Artist Taught Me To Love My Vision

At the time, I didn't realise I was creating my life like a work of art or, indeed, that by deciding to walk my talk, I was stepping into the shoes of a Life Artist. Looking back, I can see she brought me the courage to defy convention and led the way to an outstanding adventure – one that would continue to change my life forever, showing me a new way of seeing and being me.

Removing the Blinkers

It all started from a point of suffering, a crisis, as many awakenings do. I was a typical highly-stressed, career-driven teacher, freshly married and thinking that finally this was the answer to my dreams – a guarantee of happiness, love and safety.

Boy, did these dreams have a lot to live up to! One day they were whisked away, when my husband became severely ill with the dark beast that is depression. The pain, fear and very real threat of his death pushed me to question existence, challenged my faith in human nature and confronted the idea of god.

On the plus side, my exposure, my yearning for certainty, my search for happiness and love outside of myself and experiencing the very real power of the human mind (albeit the destructive side) cracked me open and woke me up.

My 'dark night of the soul' appeared one winter's eve when I was resisting another slow and agonising drive home. I loitered around, shuffling papers and preparing lessons. My perpetual denial was made incredibly easy; sacrificing your time and placing the profession before your life was a prerequisite for being a 'good to outstanding teacher'. Besides, I had to believe I was good at something.

It wasn't the drive I feared as much as the thoughts I knew would arise en route. My silence on the subject would not silence them. And when they spoke I heard the voice of the monster. Had this beast, which had clearly devoured the angelic man I'd married, also contaminated me? My perpetual busy-ness assisted in wrapping the comfort blanket of denial tightly and expertly, shutting out all possible light. Nevertheless, when the stillness came, the truth would blind me – a bit like opening the curtains too soon.

"What will I find tonight?" I worried, as swinging ropes pierced my vision. "The medication isn't working. What can I do?"

The previous night I had arrived home to Robert De Niro's Travis, in a scene from *Taxi Driver*. His beautiful hair spread across the floor and his pained eyes pleading suicide.

That evening a death did take place, and it came as predicted – unexpectedly. I remember us lying on the bed together, our arms embracing tightly, when he said: "I can't do this to you anymore. I love you so much I have to set you free."

These words, absurdly, brought a flicker of relief to my incomprehensible world. Of course, the romantic co-dependent, who thrived on the idea of love conquering all, couldn't bear it. She had failed shamefully and had no idea what to do in this situation; angry endings of betrayal and deception had been her forte. Paradoxically, this heroic gesture was far 'too' loving to comprehend. Unconditional love had left only the choice of acceptance. We made this choice together and lay supported in each other's arms for the long night ahead.

I carried on existing and found myself facing one of my biggest fears – living alone for the first time. Then, one sunny July evening, I came home from work and sat on my sumptuous sofa, surveying my fabulous new kitchen, gorgeous hardwood floor and heaps of sparkly accessories and I realised I still wasn't happy. What was wrong with me? I had created all this and even had a caring new man to fill the love gap. But there was still a gap... I just wasn't satisfied. I was living on autopilot, blindly wrapping up the pieces of one shattered dream and disguising it by sticking random bits of tinsel on the top.

I took a desperate breath and sat silently for a while. Then I heard a magical question rise from my weak, whispering soul: "What would I do if I was told I had six months to live?" The answer surprised me: "Well, I certainly wouldn't be sitting here, working all the hours god sends, and for what?"

I told myself I'd stop waiting and start living. I'd sell up, travel the world and ensure everyone I loved knew it. With these thoughts came a flutter of energy I now recognise as 'catching the flow of life'. It's the energy of possibility, empowerment and creativity. It's golden.

And so, I did just that. I sold up, packed up, had my home on my back and embarked on a round the world journey. This turned out to be a priceless experience, a precious gift of kindness and love that I bestowed on myself without guilt or shame.

My mind did try to squash it with tasty morsels of fearmongering, a juicy dose of doubt, and many 'what ifs?'. Normally that would have been enough for me to put it off and say, "One day..." But now I heard another voice, the voice of my Life Artist, saying: "Just do it." With this action a pattern was broken.

Answering the Call

I planned my journey by choosing all the amazing places I was curious to see and the magical things I'd dreamt of experiencing as a child. I connected with all the possibilities that made me squeal: "Oooh I'd love to do that." I honoured my heart.

Hitting the shores of a South Pacific island to the sound of song and tribal clapping, I stepped into Fiji time. The coral reef, connection with Nature and timeless reality melted my heart. I was actually enjoying being with me. I relaxed for the first time in years. Now, don't get me wrong, I thought I'd been relaxing every weekend with a glass of wine and my feet up! But this quality of relaxation was like nothing I could remember. I relaxed my grip enough to listen to myself, to see what I was holding onto and spent enough time with myself to create a new relationship. This was to be the start of a beautiful love affair (although it can still be rocky at times!).

After cuddling koalas in Oz, I finally touched the soil of India. This was where I ended up fulfilling the old cliché and 'found myself'. Or perhaps more accurately, I listened, rediscovered and took a good look. I had a hunch before I'd even begun my travels that this was going to be a special place for me. I had wanted to go to India for many years and didn't really know why. I thought it was because I was a bit of a hippy chick at heart and loved to shop!

This country was unlike anything I had experienced before and yet I felt as if I had arrived home. My eager and tentative steps came to symbolise all she has to offer: she is a cultural paradox full of diversity and contrast. Beautiful saris flutter in the dirty streets, the farting monks text on their mobiles. I was forced to cover my shoulders and expose my heart.

India holds up a dusty mirror to who you are. If you are brave enough to wipe off the dust and look at the contrast that is you, she will inspire grand change with humbleness and gratitude. And, ironically, amongst her chaos, she instils balance, wholeness and peace. The only place you can find peace in India is within!

I simultaneously love her and hate her. She will accept you, take you high and make you cry. She can be guaranteed to hand you what you need, although it may not be what you think you need, and there is an adventure to be had around every chai stall.

If you embrace her she will show you how to lift the veil shrouding your heart. And she offers you an abundance of tools and experiences to enable you to do it. She asks you to accept, to trust, be courageous and guides you on an invigorating journey of ever-increasing awareness. It can be a bumpy ride that is best taken with an attitude of curiosity and a huge dose of humour and playfulness. Just one auto rickshaw journey will require all of these qualities!

Unleashing the Life Artist

I started my journey in the gentle South with its swaying palm trees. Tasting the sweet aroma of cardamom with every sticky breath, I was intoxicated by the nourishing, relaxing rhythm. One day I was taking a nonchalant stroll through the dusty roads of Varkala when I came across a sign saying, "reiki healing".

"Hmm, I already had a massage yesterday, so perhaps I'll try that today," I thought. And so I found myself lying in a basic, tatty room with the magical scent of incense forcefully purifying my nasal pathways. Little did I know that this was to become the powerful scent which now invokes the familiar friend within.

The sound of chanting and the drifting scent set the scene for expectation. I closed my eyes and wondered what was about to happen.

"It's not as good as the massage yesterday," I thought after a while. "What a waste of money… she's not even touching me. I've been conned."

But I lay back and let it happen anyway. When the healer's hands moved over my heart chakra I felt an overwhelming nurturing energy; it was almost unbearably loving and physically tugged on my chest. I couldn't control the wet pain seeping from my eyes… what a relief!

After the treatment, the wise lady divulged much about myself and my life, offering guidance for healing if I wished to take it. I was amazed at this extraordinary experience, although, I thought little more about it until I found myself sitting next to a beautiful Israeli girl on the bus to Pushkar, a holy town in Rajasthan. Talking with her I discovered she had completed her reiki training in the Himalayas; she positively glowed while raving about her healing journey. A seed was planted.

My journey through Rajasthan first took me to the fairytale city of Udaipur, with its mixed flavour of Mughal and Rajasthani architecture and gleaming palaces. The magical atmosphere of this city indulged my fantasy. Artisan craftspeople, peacocks and elephants drew upon the India I had imagined and I felt anything was possible.

After my morning chai I took a stroll with the intention of finding a jeweller who could make my designs for me. A hand-painted necklace depicting Hindu god Ganesh, encircled by emeralds and rubies, beckoned me into a shop. Inside I found a meditating Jain surrounded by books. I greeted him with a smile and a "Namaste" and gazed around at the treasure chest I had entered. The energy in the room was of gentle peace and the now familiar scent of incense was welcoming and homely.

For some reason, I felt very lonely and sad. I missed my family and my old life and I burst into uncontrollable tears.

"Not again," I thought. "What's wrong with me? It's humiliating."

The poor man was very concerned for my welfare, offering me a listening ear while pouring the chai. We drank abundantly as I sobbed out my story apologetically. He shared tales of Jainism, advocating its importance. The principles of Jainism are simple and kindly: all living things are equal and to practise non-violence to all. "Don't kill the fly," he said as I waved it away from my tasty chai.

His aim was to transcend the physical: "Bodily pleasures and passions are a distraction and should be kept under control with meditation," he instructed.

I wasn't sure about that bit, although the altruistic and compassionate nature of Jainism appealed to me.

He advised me to meditate and explore philosophy as he discussed the idea of absolute truth, reality and perception.

"Meditation will help you to see. Come back tomorrow for a lesson."

I seized his invitation and was introduced to the power of the chakra system. After some regular practice I opened to the energy; I became more sensitive to the subtleties and learnt how to listen to and hear energy. I found myself becoming less emotional. I was also introduced to his wife and children and invited to attend a wedding with them. This lavish affair blew me away and the sound system blew my eardrums. Floating saris glistened as the dancing girls took pride of place. I was particularly grateful to experience such a beautiful, playful and ostentatious occasion.

The next morning, I went to the shop for my customary meditation practice. Waiting sleepily, cross-legged on the floor, I settled easily into my breathing. As I began to relax and open up, I felt a light force touching my root chakra. Was this Kundalini rising, I wondered... something certainly was. The pressure became firmer and I wasn't quite sure what to do. I opened my eyes.

"What are you doing?" I demanded.

"You want this; I can feel it in your energy," was his useless reply. I left outraged and disappointed.

I couldn't believe he had destroyed my trust in him and everything I'd learnt. I left feeling my illuminating experience was tainted forever. A few days later, though, on the bumpy bus to Pushkar, I thought about this incident and realised I had a choice about how I labelled it and stashed it away in my memory. Condemning the whole experience as fake didn't sit well with me. I felt different. It dawned on me that I could change my perception. The meditation practice really had created a shift in me, the wedding was a wonderful sight to behold and our philosophical chats had left me with profound understanding. I could also keep myself safe and handle a formidable situation. I could trust myself.

This was just an ordinary man who decided to push boundaries. In doing so, he betrayed himself and his authenticity. This wasn't my stuff... it was his. I wasn't responsible for his behaviour... he was. Why should I let it tarnish all of my delightful experiences? I arrived in Pushkar feeling chilled and capable.

The following day, I was sitting having a chai and met a

modern British Indian traveller from London. We shared parallel stories, both grieving the loss of our broken dreams. This chance meeting opened up possibilities and experiences that fuelled my transformation. His male Indian descent and fluent Hindi opened doors for him and provided me, as a Western female travelling alone, with privileged insight into a deeper realm.

I tasted the lives of the Sadhus and was welcomed into their tented home, perched precariously on the edge of the roadside, as they proudly extended their hospitality in the traditional Indian manner: sharing food and stories. They chopped fresh vegetables with rusty knives and one Baba (who carried a kitten in his pocket and had intense soul-revealing eyes) told of his reason for renunciation of the life he once knew and explained his quest for the spiritual. His motivation was also because of a broken heart; he was in love with a Muslim woman and he was Hindu.

"This love affair cannot happen in this lifetime and I accept this is not my path," he said matter-of-factly. He decided to dedicate his life to Brahman. I thought his detached emotion around the subject was strange and revealing. This weirdly painted man, dressed in orange robes, was not so dissimilar to me. I don't think we looked that different either; my hair felt like it was about to turn to dreadlocks and I am still quite partial to the vibrancy of orange! At this moment, the necessity of acceptance was made paramount to me in more ways than one.

Reclaiming Beauty

The next day my Londoner friend introduced me to his reiki master: a serene, powerful-looking man with white robes, a long black beard and kind eyes. He looked like a stereotypical Indian guru. We discussed life, spirituality and reiki, and the next thing I knew I was having my first attunement for reiki level one healing. Coming to it this way, with no real expectation, helped me connect to its power, and let it do its thing. There's definitely something about childlike faith and curiosity.

Before the attunement we talked of the power of reiki and I was told it would increase my connection with the cosmic energy that is nature.

"All you need for reiki is love, pureness of heart and intention. Reiki heals all areas of your life," he said. "It will change you forever. A new world will open up, one you want and require. You will develop psychic ability, intuition, your health, relationships, work environment, friends' circle and income will all change for the better."

"I'm not sure I want everything to change?" I said, voicing the concern that was creeping up inside.

"Reiki will take you on a journey of enlightenment. You can go as far or as little as you please," was his reply.

"A grand promise," I thought, with both scepticism and hope.

Tentatively, I sat on a chair in the dark room, both feet placed firmly on the ground; the coolness of the stone was comforting to my bare feet. I watched the metal bathroom door, peeling with rust. My nostrils welcomed my old friend incense as the master smudged the room and chanted. With my eyes closed, I was left with my breath. There was stillness for what seemed to be an age. A buzzing energy at the top of my crown started to tickle, a bit like rubbing a balloon on your hair to make it stand up on end. It was nice. I relaxed. I began to bliss out and remained in this state, offering loving drops of gratitude from my eyes. I both melted and expanded.

After giving thanks, I was instructed to open my eyes and put out my hands and ask for reiki energy to come. I hastily wiped my hot and sweaty palms on my kurta and instantly felt a mighty heat flow through them.

"Wow this is weird, like magic," I thought, and smiled to myself.

I remained in that state of joyful happiness for the next two days. I was loved up and highly alert, walking on air, entirely at peace, like a cat on catnip. I saw only love, and that was what I received from all I encountered. The only previous experience that came vaguely near to this feeling was taking ecstasy. Yet, this euphoric bliss was clean, serene, pure and masterfully balanced. The tap was well and truly turned on and flowing wildly: it was abundant. I was totally loved.

Through dutiful healing practice the energy within me balanced. And like all euphoric experiences there has to be a comedown. In this case it came in the form of conscious awareness, authentic healing, self-actualisation and a whole set of positive new beliefs. I was offered the mirror of life and asked to look inside. Although often uncomfortable, for the first time ever I could see beyond the surface, push through the judgment, pain and distorted perception to unearth the hidden truth: a reflection of love.

Your Life Artist Is Your North Star Guiding You To Rise and Shine

There are artists who transform the sun into a yellow spot,
but there are others who, thanks to their art and intelligence,
transform a yellow spot into the sun.
Pablo Picasso

Here Comes Your Sun

What would life be like if you looked at your reflection in the mirror each morning with a Life Artist's loving perception, asking how can I add new beauty, meaning and purpose to my day? With this understanding as your default, life is empowering and precious; you get to live life like it's golden.

When I was plunged into darkness, I instinctively ran to the sun. My journey of discovery guided me to sunny shores and this was no coincidence. The sun is a healer and bringer of light. The rising sun of hope has been revered and worshipped as the source of creation here on Earth since time began. The sun is an alchemic symbol that represents the completing of the Great Work and holds an important place in our culture, myth and ritual. We only need to take a trip through art history to see its inspiration on the creative mind. The sun is the bestower of light and life and the keeper of wisdom.

How do you feel when I tell you that you have a sun to shine, a Great Work to complete and this is where you will discover your beauty?

There's a wonderful Japanese tale about the illuminating Sun Goddess Amaterasu who, to cut a long story short, had an argument with her brother the Storm God, retreated in protest to a cave, and plunged the world into darkness. I'm assuming this also put great pressure on her brother, the Moon. The other 800 gods tried everything they could to lure her out, bringing crowing cocks and even hanging a mirror and jewels on a tree in front of the cave.

One of the female gods started dancing to entertain the patiently waiting tribe of deities; as she pirouetted her robe slipped off, causing the tribe to laugh in excitement. Amaterasu heard the laughter and wanted to know why they could be so joyful while the world was plunged into darkness; she was told that outside the cave there was a deity more illustrious than she. Her curiosity got the better of her and she peeped out, saw her reflection in the mirror, heard the cocks crow, and was drawn out from the cave.

A little word of warning here... if you're anything like me, you might become distracted by the crowing cocks as you peep out of your cave, crediting them for your light. While there's a lot of merriment to be had with cocks that crow, remembering they only crow because you shine is important. Seeing your authentic reflection is the only solution to coming out of the cave.

Coming Out of Your Cave – Alchemy For Life

Illuminating and seeing your reflection is a lifelong and powerful process – it is alchemy for life – a committed practice of turning life's lead into gold and living life "like it's golden". With the daily unfolding of your authentic truth you can harmonise with your natural place in creation; you can be and see 'all that you are' and magnify your part in the star-studded mosaic.

How do you go about turning your 'lead into gold'?

This book offers you many ways to practically turn your lead into gold; they all help to purify and unify your energy system by bringing your mind and body's vibration into alignment to resonate more effectively with your co-creator. This will help you to clearly hear your creative call and receive the guidance you need to complete your Great Work.

Transmuting your energy can be messy work; recognising and sifting through your darkest or unknown parts and releasing the lingering energy of habits, behaviours, belief systems and past events that no longer serve you productively, takes awareness, surrender, trust and courage – it's not for the faint-hearted! However, it is only by doing this that you can spot and fully integrate your 'golden essence' and reflect the beauty of your true nature.

Your life is 'the Great Work' bringing you to wholeness if you let it. When you take the risk to hold up your sun and shine it, you become the luminary lighting up yourself, your life, and the world.

The Life Artist's Way

The Life Artist builds bridges between worlds so she can move between them and provide new pathways for others to do the same.

Being a Life Artist is a state of heart and mind, a lifestyle, and a daily choice.

It's a commitment you make to express yourself and create more beautiful moments in your life, to be the flower of life that you naturally are. You will be asked to show up to life, implement your vision with heart-led decisions, and share your wisdom with the world.

Your Life Artist will show you your authentic reflection. She will lead you to nourishment and teach you how to reconnect to your creative cosmic powers, from the roots up, so that you can rise and shine.

Creating your shining freedom is an empowering habit that ultimately becomes your destiny. You will find your tribe of sun sisters who are flowering in the same field as you and be supported in your purpose.

I won't pretend being a Life Artist is easy. It's risky to follow your heart's desire and sometimes we get burned and trampled upon. Remembering that the sun still shines when it rains, or when we can't see her at night, helps me in challenging times. I've discovered that it's more dangerous to believe in the illusion of 'staying safe', because 'staying safe' disconnects you from the power of your true purpose, and all that you can be in your lifetime. Some flowers may well get trampled in the process of blossoming, but is it not better to die a natural death while experiencing purpose?

Are you ready to take the risk, step into your light, let it move through your entire being and become a Life Artist?

The Life Artist's Craft

Before moving forward to the work and play of uncovering your sun, it's a good idea to spend some time learning your craft. There are two simple yet essential skills you need to embody your Life Artist and feel fully confident in her shoes. The first of these is 'the way of being' and the second is 'the way of seeing'.

The Way of Being

The Life Artist's hidden talent is that they know they need to be both the art and the artist. This way of being is a highly transformative and empowering skill. It expands your perception and shapes your reality so that you can recognise the purpose to bring to each day.

How does this dual position actually work?

Well, there is some science behind this art and it's called the Observer Effect, where the actual act of observation alters what is being observed. By looking at yourself you have the ability to change and learn about you. Have you heard the expression 'shed some light on it'? Well, that's literally what you are doing when you observe. This effect liberates you and facilitates a two-way flow of energy where information is absorbed and reflected back. This is a valuable tool for the Life Artist. You can see the choices available to you, shape how you want to fit in the world, and move towards wholeness.

Separating the artist from their art is a difficult thing to do and an interesting idea to explore. Where does the essence of the creator end and the form of creation begin? Or does the relationship only change from the vantage point we take? What happens in the mystical space between the two? Will we ever really know?

To answer all of these profound questions in depth would take another book, although you will begin to form your answers to them as you develop your craft as a Life Artist.

Let's delve a little deeper into the big questions of what constitutes art and what an artist is.

What Is Art?

Art is the language of souls, offering ways to share, connect with and experience each other.

There are many debates as to what constitutes 'art' – commercial art, fine art, the expressive arts and even children's art. For the purpose of this book I use the term 'art' to include all art forms: dance, theatre, acting, writing, design, painting, music, sculpture, gardening. Any creative act can produce art, but what makes it stand out as a great work of art?

A great work of art asks questions: Who am I? What am I? What am I expressing? What am I communicating? What is my purpose?

Art connects colour, form, shape, pattern, sound and movement in a unique way to evoke emotion, reveal truths, and communicate the artist's intentions.

As art you will become a provocateur and incite souls with your questions. Your friends and family will notice your radiant beauty and begin to ask questions about their own purpose in the world. And so, the big mosaic pattern lights up and continues to expand.

What Is an Artist?

The artist has worn many faces over the ages and has been seen as a maker of things, a genius, a sage, a tortured, starving vagabond, and a 'no proper job time-waster'. They have been revered as the bearers of tradition and spiritual masters. As well as being accused of selling out to the masses, they are convention-breakers, healers of the earth, political anarchists, idealists and creatives.

The term artist covers all the creative disciplines from actor, musician, literary writer, dancer and visual artist. And the thing that unites them is their calling. This calling is the soul's voice.

The energy of love is the driving force behind any great art, and as an artist, you can use it to push through your resistance and provide you with a vision you love. All artists must love their vision to create.

As a Life Artist, you repeatedly co-create forms with spirit, and you and your life also become this form. You become both the known and the unknown, the writer and the book, the actor and the director, the painter and the canvas. This skill gets really exciting because you can create an imaginative vision of yourself and experience the mysterious world in new ways. When you embrace this 'way of being' you will grow to love your vision of yourself, feel empowered to answer your calling, and discover your story of greatness.

Now you have become familiar with the transformative craft of 'being' we can explore the second essential skill of the Life Artist – the 'way of seeing'.

The Way of Seeing

The way you look at yourself matters; it affects who you become. How many of us truly notice how we are looking at ourselves and our lives? Instead, we go through life anticipating what we are going to see, how we will react, and often miss out on our potential.

All artists have a particular way of seeing. They look for space. They see the world as it really is – a mass of shapes, colours and forms – and in doing so, they tend to see the bigger picture or more of the whole. They adopt the eagle's eye. They can then observe and use all the space available to them, forming new ways of working with the objects already in the scene.

Imagine what it would be like if there was no space between the musician's notes. We wouldn't recognise it as music – it would be one continuous noise. To create beautiful art, the musician must see space to shape a melody, rhythm and harmony. The director must see space to shape meaning with dialogue and action, and the painter must see space to shape image.

When a non-artist sees the world, they have a tendency to focus only on the images or action and create concepts out of them. These well-worn habits of seeing limit the potential available to them.

Spotting Your Potential

You create your life in the same way you would a piece of art and space is the bar where potential hangs out waiting to be picked up. It stands to reason that if you're wearing your blinkers and are only focusing on the action or images in your life – getting the children to school, worrying about having enough money to last the month, or obsessing over the new line that's appeared on your forehead – you're not seeing the entire space available to you, and miss out on a divine date with potential.

How many times have you screamed to yourself, "I just need some space, any space will do"? But you link space with time, and with your hectic life, choose not to see the space available to you. You intuitively know space will provide you with your answer. This is your soul guiding you to make time to listen to yourself.

If we choose not to make space and ignore our soul's guidance, life becomes harder and we can easily feel like worn-out victims waiting to be rescued from a repetitious tragedy. We grow weaker, blinded by life's hectic clutter; we become tired and disillusioned with life.

Crafting your 'way of seeing' opens your cosmic eye, giving you the eagle's perception, and drops the drawbridge to the many spaces or worlds available to you, revealing that they are focus dependent, rather than time dependent. You are invited to take your pleasure... enter the space, and get frisky with potential. It is here you will learn to walk with a foot in both worlds – where the physical and mystical realms merge and the impossible starts to become 'I'm possible'.

How To Unveil Your Original

What Are You Prepared to Accept as Your Original?

As a Life Artist you have made the choice to awaken your spirit and when you make this simple choice it's like a massage for your soul – can you hear the sighs of relief and pleasure? Take a rest, bask for a moment in this life-changing decision and relax...

The question to ask yourself when working through the following section is "What am I prepared to accept as my original?" This question will help you to deepen your understanding of your authentic nature.

Let's take a look at how we can go about this.

Show Up: The Life Artist's Starting Point

You need to be willing to step outside the cave and burst from your pod before you can see your authentic self. Showing up to life or any creative project requires you to put your heart and soul into it. This means bringing all your presence, attention and energy to the moment, to be all you can be, warts 'n' all!

Opening up to your authenticity requires you to be vulnerable and you will feel resistance. This resistance is a bit like a painful yoga stretch because you are expanding. I urge you to breathe through your resistance and take this risk. As Anais Nin said: "Life shrinks or expands in proportion to one's courage." It is only with courage that you can start to uncover your original. There is no hiding from it; to show up requires courage.

Take the Risk

Just do it! Make the space to answer the whispers of your soul. Start with a small step if that feels more comfortable. There's no need to go in with full guns blazing and pack your job in, sell your home, and travel the world – although I thoroughly recommend it! This risk will bring you integrity. You will create a state where your authentic self is naturally expressed and loved. You will begin to blossom and flourish.

Trust That Life Loves You

This is tough if you have experienced any kind of abuse, betrayal or are feeling victimised. It's often a stumbling block for my clients as it was for myself. Bringing compassion, kindness and love into your daily actions and communicating regularly with your co-creator will build your trust and help it to grow.

Do be aware that it's easy to fall into thinking life is going to magically be a bed of roses now that you're flowering. Trust doesn't mean that everything will go exactly as you want, it means having faith that your truth is expanding from your situation. I was at a point where I was angry at life, I felt my co-creator had betrayed me and I said f**k off to the world. As I've said, I didn't know I was having an Alchemy Moment. Remembering we will also receive the uncomfortable Alchemy Moments because we need to keep growing and to keep in alignment with the great mosaic will keep our trust strong in tough times.

P.S. Don't trust a monkey... practise discernment with them! As I was writing the above paragraph, a wild monkey sneaked into my room and grabbed my bright orange Zincite crystal from the desk. I was obviously putting my heart, soul, and full awareness into my writing! I didn't even hear or feel it get so close to me. Luckily this crystal wasn't tasty, so he dropped it on the way out.

This exhilarating experience has also brought my soul joy, which leads me nicely onto the next step of awakening your Life Artist's spirit.

Soul Joy: The Life Artist's Usherette

In the theatre, the usherette will shine a light to guide you to your seat. This is exactly what your soul's joy does. Our souls are unique to us and they know what's good for us and what lessons we need to experience. They carry an imprint of the star-studded mosaic and our role in it.

Your soul's joy will lead you to your gifts, your lessons and your unique essence – all you need to do is listen.

How Do You Hear Your Soul's Voice?

Your soul uses a particular language that you are already able to hear and will refine as you journey through the chapters of the book. It's also the language of artists: inspiration, intuition and imagination.

Inspiration Is Your Map

Your soul will lead you to fertile ground by dangling sweet carrots of inspiration throughout your day. Make time to align with your soul as it communes through symbols and signs. If you feel an intuitive hunch or nudge, see, or hear something repeatedly – three times or more is often how I know my soul is speaking – then follow this up. It will lead you to soul joy.

A little word of warning: Don't believe everything you think!

Often we think we know best and avoid our soul's nudges because we are too busy to take that walk in nature, or don't want to hear what it has to say to us about the new job promotion we've committed to. When this happens, go into your heart and be still; get in touch with your feelings, listen and remember you don't see the whole picture, but your soul does. Your soul will reward you with incredible ideas and synchronicities that will guide your consciousness and move you towards wholeness.

Intuition Is Your Compass

Most of us hear and feel our intuition, yet few of us trust and act on it, because it doesn't offer us certainty. As the great Picasso once said: "To know what you're going to draw, you have to begin drawing." Acting on your intuition will bring surprising connections and impressions that don't feel as if they arise from you. These are the interesting ones to follow... they are your soul speaking.

If you haven't a clue where to start, begin by thinking back to when you were a child. What did you always dream of doing? Perhaps you always wanted to sing in a band. Book some lessons, or form a band with your friends, do some karaoke, anything that squeezes those tears of joy from your soul. Soul joy will become a familiar guide that leads you to your purpose in the most extraordinary ways.

As a child, I used to dream repeatedly of galloping white horses. Last year I started noticing images of white horses everywhere – on the Internet, TV, even in the dentist's waiting room. I discovered they were from the Camargue region of south-west France, so I travelled there to photograph them. Something inside me stirred when I saw them, as though we recognised each other. The horses' intuitive nature, and their love, sensitivity and support towards me was tangible. The sublime experience I had with them provided me with a profound soul healing and it led me to extreme joy. Now there's no way I could have known how this experience would be for me, but I followed the hunches and nudges from soul and was blessed with a beautiful experience way beyond my dreams. I also have a stunning set of images capturing the sublime energy of this moment. One was hand-picked to be included in an online article, where they said, *"the image has a unique quality making it food for your creative soul."*

In the words of the great poet Rumi: "Let the beauty we love be what we do." And that is exactly what your soul will inspire. Your job on earth is to discover and express your timeless beauty, shining the light of your soul until your last breath is taken.

Imagination Is Your Portal

Our minds have an extraordinary ability to imagine – to create pictures, we use it daily to build our lives. This is a powerful gift that we often brush off as insignificant fantasy, which is foolish because what we can imagine, we can create and experience: it defines us. The more clearly we can hold our creative visions in our mind's eye, the more likely they are to manifest.

You see, when you enter the magnificent world of your creative imagination – bringing with you awareness, feeling, and clear intent – your mind begins to illustrate what you experience into a form. It starts to paint a picture with your feelings and beliefs.

How your mind illustrates your experience is a colourful masala of how and what you think, feel and believe, your previous experiences and your environment. We can all dive into this well of unlimited creativity. Potentially we can create absolutely anything we want in our lives, as long as we can imagine and believe it. But we are limited by how we experience it in our body.

Using our imaginations, we can fly into the cosmos and kiss the Sun quite easily. To take our body with us would be much more difficult, if not impossible, to do. It does not make the experience any less real to us if our bodies are not there – this is why anxiety has such an intense impact on people's lives today – often leading to phobias and panic attacks. Your world is a projection of your internal state, which is why it's important to use your imagination consciously.

Letting your imagination run away with you is powerful; whether you imagine the worst or the best scenarios, it will directly influence your visual perception and what you see in the future. Joel Pearson established from his research on "The Functional Impact of Mental Imagery on Conscious Perception" that "imagining something changes vision both while you are imagining it and later on. The results showed that even a single instance of imagery can tilt how you see the world one way or another, dramatically, if the conditions are right."

How Does This Influence Us as Co-Creators?

Your imagination forms the basis for creating with spirit; it activates the co-creative forces of the universe for you to accomplish your Great Work.

We know our imaginations are powerful; we create our reality with them, but there is a little more to it. Even though it is 'potentially' possible for us to create anything we want, I do believe there are some things that are not open for us to experience in this lifetime because there is also an intention for our life that is governing the experiences we have throughout it. We are already in the process of creating experiences in which we, ourselves, have chosen to participate. Following your soul's guiding light will draw you, like a moth to a flame, to your life-expanding experiences, urging you to become whole.

Fear – The Life Artist's Creative Excuse

When you awaken the spirit of your Life Artist you will approach life with a conscious creative perception and your experience of life will change. It is natural that you will at times feel vulnerable and fearful.

All artists come up with excuses for not getting stuff done and fear is the creative excuse of the Life Artist. When you experience fear and resistance, see them as positive signs: you are heading in the right direction but try to move through your fear without getting stuck there. Becoming aware of when you are slipping into fear, and knowing how to transform it, will keep your heart open so you can create from an authentic space.

The energy of fear is sneaky, heavy, constricting, and even paralysing at times. It feels very real for us but fear is an emotional energy. With our powerful imaginations in action we imagine it in our minds and feel it in our bodies and so look for a form to attach it to. Once you've recognised you are stuck in fear, you can transform your fearful energy into a liberating state.

How To Transform Fear

Fear is actually about your ability to receive and there are many ways you can relate to fear to transform the energy into a more productive state.

Start by transforming fear from the space of a still heart (without emotion). I don't mean not feeling. Without emotion means waiting for the waves to settle and taking the eagle's viewpoint of the situation. This brings discernment.

A simple way I use to transform the energy of fear is by asking myself if I should transform the fear into courage, pleasure or respect. Courage leads to action, pleasure leads to gratitude, and respect leads to acceptance.

If the fear is something I can do something about – such as standing up for myself if I'm being bullied – then that fear energy can be transformed into courage and appropriate action.

If I am fearing eating a piece of chocolate, I can transform the energy into pleasure. I can stop resisting, say "yes" and take pleasure in the chocolate. Or I say "no" and have gratitude for my choice. Either way I'm not stuffing the energy of fear into my body.

If it's a fear of a natural disaster that I cannot do anything about, like a tsunami, then transforming the energy into respect brings acceptance and discernment.

Whichever way, it's important to let the fear energy express itself in a new productive form so you can move on to receive life.

Now is a good time to have a pause and ask yourself the question at the beginning, "What am I prepared to accept as my truth, my original?"

10 benefits of being a Life Artist

It's your time to be seen; be ready as Your Life Artist will:

1. Teach you how to love yourself – the artist loves her art.
2. Teach you how to defy the nay-sayers and critics.
3. Show you how to rise up and speak your truth.
4. Guide you to finding your tribe of like-minded Sun Sisters.
5. Reveal your vision, provide the guidance and passion to create it, and help you to offer it to the world.
6. Uncover your authentic voice and creative spark.
7. Encourage you to use your life to inspire.
8. Teach you that a human spiritual experience is an essential part of living.
9. Instil the courage to risk the loss of belonging and the fear of loneliness, in order to be true to yourself.
10. Open pathways to the spiritual realm and become intimate with your Creatrix.

The Creatrix

Now that your Life Artist's spirit is raring to go, you can call on your Creatrix.

Whenever you start to do anything creative, sooner or later you will come across your inner critic. Affirming the presence of your Creatrix is the only way to dim the voice of the inner critic.

Your Creatrix is your archetypal creative guide. She communicates esoteric information to you and will help with all of your creative endeavours. She is your spirit muse offering herself to you for exploration. Your relationship with her is intimate, intuitive, private, primeval and never-ending. She offers you both inspiration and a means to express that inspiration.

The Creatrix is spontaneous, flighty, wild, reckless, sensual, messy, and sensitive. Her body expands with thrill and excitement, yet her extreme sensitivity requires encouragement and time to reveal her offerings fully. She must play. Her playful energy is highly charged, and she asks you to look beyond with tempting colour and a curious fascination. She makes the impossible, possible. Let her dance with you.

Your Creatrix is your access point to another world. A reality where dreams exist and manifest. Beckoned with intent, she simultaneously lives in both worlds, and shows you how to do the same.

Attract her with relaxation, play, trust, and experience her fully. She is in dialogue with your soul and can communicate your desires. The more you call her, the longer she will stay. Her powers are sacred. Give her permission to experiment and lose herself and she will be content.

She will ask you to trust in her creative power and lose yourself in creation, so you can experience creation fully. You will dance with creation. It is the dance between giving creative power to the external world and taking the creative power internally.

The Creatrix is an elusive flow, and weaves busily behind the scenes to illuminate. She can create order from chaos and bring life to form with her breath. She unfolds and harmonises the incompatible, ignites the imagination, and opens a portal – your power point leading to your expanded consciousness.

This is the place that will lead you to retain your power. In this sacred domain, you can express your uniqueness, and yet become one with humanity. Your energy vibrations raise and your powers open. You can dream and manifest your dreams into reality.

How To Summon Your Creatrix

One very powerful way to make a connection with your Creatrix is to create a piece of artwork to honour her. The art form itself acts as a container to hold her spirit and becomes a living bridge between your world and the energetic world where she resides. You are consciously bringing her energy into form. I did a painting of my Creatrix. She is called Flourish. I made her as beautiful as I possibly could. She now hangs above my desk and I draw on her energy for many creative projects. You can use any type of form you wish, write a poem, create lyrics, paint, craft, draw, knit or sculpt. The difference between this and 'just' creating a piece of art is your focus, intention and the sacred space you create.

Prepare Your Space: This means clearing the energy in your physical space to do sacred work and work with divine energy. I do this by smudging the room with sage and placing a reiki symbol in each corner of the room, with a clear intent in my mind that I am preparing the room for soul work. What you are actually doing by smudging the room and clearing is removing any previous or unwanted energy.

Call in Spirit or Energy: I use the Shamanic technique of calling in spirit to oversee and work with me. There are also other techniques to use. You can ask your spirit guides, the angels, your god, reiki energy, nature or the cosmos to oversee the connection. The important thing is to ask for guidance from something outside of yourself as energetically this will enable you to bridge the worlds.

Make Your Connection with Her: I do this with a shamanic journey; this is the most powerful way I have found to receive this type of information from energy. For example, I will set the intent to journey to meet my Creatrix. I will either use my shamanic drum to journey and enter a trance-like state or I will lie down and set my intent to meet her and start visioning. There are many ways to make your connection. You can also use your breath to still yourself, take a walk in nature, or meditate. What is important is to hold your intent, clarity and focus to meet your Creatrix and to create a deeply relaxed state of consciousness, as this will help you to sense and listen to her energy. It's a good idea to have a journal handy and write down any impressions, visions or feelings you have afterwards; this will help to manifest the energy further. Continue to hold the space and try not to break your state; popping to the loo or going to make a coffee before you start your artwork can break or weaken your connection.

Create: Give yourself plenty of time. Allow yourself to once again drift into a trance-like state; as you create you may find it helpful to play some music that is specifically designed to take your brainwaves into theta frequency. Shamanic drumming will do this; you can find downloads of this type on my website. Trust, play and experiment, remembering to hold your intent in mind throughout.

Give Thanks: When you have completed your art, spend some time looking at it and holding it, stating and imbuing your intent clearly again. Give thanks to spirit and to your Creatrix for joining you. Place your artwork in a beautiful space where it can be honoured.

Snippets of Wisdom

My art
makes
The earth's
heart beat

Now let's celebrate with a banquet, and feast on the Cosmic Powers of nature, energy and beauty. These will plump up your roots of existence and sculpt them to illuminate the exquisite art of you. Nature feeds your belonging, Energy feeds your quality of life, and Beauty feeds your soul.

Let's explore the finest ways to devour these tasty morsels.

Chapter 3

Nature As Master

Let's paint a picture....

Beautiful Connections

The morning sun peeps out from behind the coconut tree, offering fresh light and inspiration. The backdrop of a Robinson Crusoe-like seashore springs to life with the buzzing of dragonflies and the chattering of fishermen. Every morning these men gather on the beach. To feed their families they rely on the sun rising, the wood from the trees to carve their boat, the waves of the sea to carry their vessel, and the four winds to direct it.

The heron, a hero amongst his kind, the crazy crow with all her babies, and the lazy kingfisher have all mastered the art of perfect timing: they know exactly when to fly into the scene as the fishermen offload the unwanted catch of the day.

As well as providing the air for the old cook to breathe, the surrounding palm trees playfully drop their coconuts with guttural rhythm while she does the traditional dinner dance. Combined with the harmonising sound of the soothing turquoise ocean and the cardamom-infused air, the most exquisite image is sculpted – a true masterpiece... an authentic, living work of art.

I am also part of this picture: I am a work of art, living in an organic work of art. It's within this image I am inspired to find words for this page.

The pale-skinned foreigner, with sun-kissed hair and freaky freckles, sits on a yoga mat on the floor and taps away on the computer keys. She gazes wistfully at the scene below her, wondering if the dolphin will make an appearance today, and which fish she will eat for dinner. She uses the art form of writing to transport this experience to you.

Reclaiming Connections

Choose only one Master – Nature.
Rembrandt

Nature is the Life Artist's studio space, your haven, a place to collect your thoughts and seek inspiration. Within this incredible space is also your mother, your friend, your teacher, your doctor; all wrapped neatly into the one Master you should model on Earth.

Why Reclaim Our Connection with Nature?

The first step to understanding yourself as a work of art is to find an inspiring teacher. Nature designs life for a living and is the greatest teacher you can have: you are one of her masterpieces. By reclaiming your role in the natural world and reviving your relationship with Nature, you have access to your natural power – to all that is alive and vital. You feel a sense of belonging and your appreciation and respect grow for the diversity of all life, including your own.

This chapter will explore what she can teach us and how we can put this into practice in our lives.

As I'm scribbling these words I'm sitting in my studio space, seeking inspiration from the great Master. I'm listening to the dawn chorus, surrounded by swaying palms and the scent of flowering coffee trees. There are literally hundreds of birds singing their exclusive songs. Among them is the orange laughing thrush, the purple sunbird and, of course, the black crow. They have risen, and are showing up to life in all their glory. There is no editing, no competition or comparison between them – they exhibit a sense of belonging, simply being all they can be in this moment. By doing this they are creating the most enchanting scene for me to share with you, as well as offering a perfect analogy of what life is like for us when we work in harmony with Nature.

Can you imagine a life without a garden of stars, without inspirational sunsets, without refreshing raindrops, without galloping horses, or raging seas? Each one of these is Nature's art. You are invited daily to interact with this great work of art to communicate with it, take pleasure from it and contribute to it.

Our Garden the Shopping Mall

Nature teaches by example; she is a natural healer and invites us to step inside her to nourish ourselves with the beauty of life. Generations ago, we understood her healing powers; we went to the local shaman for our medication, hospitals had their own healing gardens and doctors would prescribe 'one week's rest by the sea'.

These days we have lost sight of nature's power and are more likely to swallow a quick fix of addictive retail therapy to ease our malady. Searching for solace in the shopping mall leaves us feeling dissatisfied; it peaks rapidly and then we need more.

Instead of empowering ourselves through nature, we are rapidly consuming her healing resources. In a desperate bid to become and possess more, building larger cities, drilling for more oil and chopping down even more trees, we are isolating ourselves and increasing our sense of lack. We have forgotten we are a part of Nature and that how we interact with her will affect us. By felling the trees we are limiting our oxygen supply, by limiting our oxygen we will take smaller breaths, by taking smaller breaths we will feel less, sense less and, above all, shorten our lifespan.

What was once seen as progressive civilisation has become a hysteria of consumption leaving us feeling disconnected and out of balance with our natural world. Nature has given us free rein to experience and create harmoniously alongside her, but we are not listening to her wisdom. We have lost sight of beauty.

How is this disconnection from nature shaping your life?

Is Your Normal Natural?

Have you ever come from a hard day at work and felt as though someone had been shaking you all day? Your instinct is to take a simple walk in Nature, hear the birdsong exploding from the trees, expose yourself to the ruggedness of the landscape, taste the sharp wind and marvel at the thrilling wild waves. The rhythm of this exquisite piece of art is natural – it's your rhythm; it soothes and stimulates your senses, eases your mind and body. You know Nature is your number one power source and sustains your life here on Earth.

Then you forget, switch off the plug, so to speak. You forget your natural and revert to your normal; you go home to a million and one chores – kids, dog, homework, cake-baking competitions – and you lose the feeling of belonging.

Our apathetic busyness stops us receiving Nature's nourishment. It's a vicious cycle... we spend less time with her and feel less energised. This separated state is completely unnatural for us, although it has become normal for many of us.

This conflicting disparity between our 'normal' everyday lives and our 'natural' state eventually leads to our spiritual and physical decline and life becomes monotonous. We feel: stressed, undernourished, empty, lethargic – as though a part of us is broken. The loneliness this produces is unbearable and becomes a breeding ground for addictions as we numb the painful sound of separateness with our favourite vices – alcohol, social media, drugs, gambling, sex, food... anything to drown out the void and feel a part of something.

Many of us are experiencing 'burnout' because we are not getting the fuel from Nature that we need to stay vibrant and alive. The distracting demands of technology, particularly our smartphones, are constantly interrupting our attention. Persistent multitasking is causing stress, increasing anxiety and inhibiting our ability to focus; it is placing too much strain on our brains and bodies and starving our spirit.

Our hectic, technology-laden lifestyles are pulling us further and further away from our natural and intricate relationship with Nature and this is weakening our roots – the very roots you need to rise up and share your art with the world.

The Chain Reaction of Apathy

Global warming, our carbon footprint, pesticides causing the massacre of the world's bees are topics in the news headlines every day. Why do we do nothing about it?

Our busy lives are turned towards what we see as more 'important' stressors: terror attacks, Brexit, banks crashing, securing a job promotion, managing the children's allergies or grabbing your sister's favourite flowers on the way to visit her in hospital where she is being treated for cancer.

All the elements above are interconnected and influence you and I directly. Simply by looking at the effect of pesticides on the world, we can see an ugly chain reaction: the bees die, your son develops allergies, your sister becomes ill with cancer – but there are no more flowers.

We are an integral part of nature, whatever we are doing (or not doing) to her, we are also doing to ourselves. The more we nurture Nature and strengthen our relationship with her, the stronger and healthier she – and we – will become.

How can we restore the balance back into our lives and our world?

What can I do?
What can you do?
What can we do?

We can rewild. Rewilding will re-establish balance in the powerful relationship that exists between you, me and the natural world, and show you how to use that power.

Rewilding

Rewilding is a term used in ecology to restore something to its natural uncultivated state where it can roam free, living harmoniously with nature. There is a wonderful example of this where endangered grey wolves were introduced back into Yellowstone National Park in the USA. The reintroduction of these top predators into the eco-system caused what's known as a tropic cascade; they shaped the behaviour of all species in that eco-system. The deer's behaviour changed and they stopped going to certain parts of the park. Forests grew in those spaces; increasing the bears, birds and berries. Beavers moved in and built dams that housed otters and so on. But most remarkably, when the balance was brought back to its natural state, the rivers changed shape. The landscape physically altered, and this also happens to us.

Our inner landscapes affect and reflect our outer landscapes, and vice versa. When we rewild ourselves and make space for our true nature, our original and authentic processes take over, releasing us from the pressure of normal and allowing us to return to our wild, natural state.

How Do We Start Rewilding?

We can start by making Nature our master.

Essentially this entire book leads you through a process of rewilding – of untaming and reclaiming your true nature. But this chapter focuses on what you can learn from your outer landscape – Nature – to reinstate the wild wisdom of your inner landscape.

Let's get started...

How Do You Keep Your Eco-System Balanced?

Here are two powerful features from the Yellowstone example that you can use straight away to restore balance:

1. Relinquish Control:

You too have an ancient wilderness within – your wild and wise landscape. You instinctively know how to flourish there and in which direction you should be growing. Just like nature, you have an inbuilt self-organisation and self-rejuvenation ability. When you relinquish control, and allow this uncultivated part of you to 'do what it will', your natural processes take over and your connection to yourself and to Nature unfold.

2. Determine Your Man-Made Predators from Your Natural Predators:

As we have seen, the natural top predator is a driving force for change in any eco-system and keeps the landscape wild; a little bit of fear keeps us healthy and growing in the right direction. However, our culture of consumption is taming our wild nature, pruning us like highly-prized Bonsai trees. One of the top predators that has evolved from this system, drives it forward, and stops us becoming authentically wild, is financial fear. This is our modern-day, man-made predator. Many of us stay in marriages or jobs because we fear the financial predator and it shapes our lives in an unnatural way, leading us further away from our wild, wise forests and ancient power. If we stop consuming as much and start creating for ourselves the man-made control begins to fall apart and leaves space for our wild beauty to take shape in our lives.

Only you can decide what your true nature is and what has been interfered with by man or over-cultivated. As the old saying goes, "You don't know what you've got till it's gone." So, the first thing you can do is to get to know what you have. You can reconnect with the wonder of nature, you can care, you can start to consciously add your own beautiful expression to the planet.

Born Belonging

We are born into this world connected to all things. We even arrive with a massive symbolic umbilical sign that reminds us of this fact. Inscribed inside the arteries is the sacred blueprint for our survival; the pattern of a tree. No kidding! The placenta and umbilical cord look as though they have been block-printed with the tree of life – nature's beautiful branding, reminding us of how to sustain our lives and vitality here on Earth. We are not only born belonging, but we are also gifted with a blueprint of how to survive.

This sense of belonging is what we yearn for in our lives, it makes us feel complete as though we have 'arrived home'. Yet we often seek it in the wrong places – relationships, jobs, vices, and end up dissatisfied when they don't fulfil our needs. Nature can show you how to feel this deep sense of belonging once again and appreciate your place in the Circle of Life.

The Circle of Life

Just like the block-printed placenta, Nature also provides us with a guide for staying connected and living a creative, harmonious and balanced way of life. She has painted this symbol everywhere; it is, of course, the circle.

The sacred circle shape represents the interconnectivity of all aspects of our being, including our connection with the natural world. Life is one big circle, a constant loop. The Sun, the Moon and the Earth are artworks acting as daily reminders that our lives are cyclical, not linear, and we, as part of the whole, follow the same patterns. Life is a circle of birth, maturity, decay, death and rebirth for all living things.

The circle unites all that it contains and holds much wisdom for the Life Artist. My drama classroom was purposely designed as an empty space with no tables or chairs. Instead of the traditional teacher standing at the front of the class set-up, we all sat in a circle and would regularly hold what's known as 'circle time', a democratic space where everyone feels safe to contribute their ideas, listen to each other and reflect. This powerful space not only bred equality and unity amongst students, but it also fostered divergent thinking.

Our brains think in two ways:

Convergent thinking – that's when you're making a judgment, analysing, criticising and evaluating something to come up with one right answer. It's logical and it's how we've been taught to think most of the time.

Divergent or creative thinking – where our imaginations are free to come up with endless possibilities in a spontaneous, collaborative and innovative manner. We equally need both these types of thinking in our daily lives, but with an educational system that places emphasis and value on convergent thinking this is usually our default approach, which diminishes our creative brain power and screens our creative choices.

The divergent thinking circle reminds us of life's many creative possibilities, it combats comparison and competition, provides a voice for difference, and invites cohesion and creative solutions. It is the Life Artist's sacred asset.

What Wild Wisdom Can You Draw from This?

The Circle of Life represents unity of all things and teaches you that all things are interrelated and an equal part of the whole. Everything depends on everything else, with the Great Spirit at the centre of all life.

Viewing your life as a simple circle helps you to:

- feel your belonging
- understand your relationship with nature
- preserve your power
- find innovative solutions and bring meaning to your

individual challenges
- and reminds you to think creatively.

The sacred circle offers us many teachings, which you can explore in a practical way in Part Two of this book.

For now, try this exercise to help you understand how you are viewing your circle of life:

Draw a circle and put a dot in the centre.

The circle is your life and the dot represents your Creator. You'll notice the circle, like the Life Artist, has neither a beginning nor an end, and so is both infinite Creation and Creator. (Interestingly a circle with a dot in it is also a symbol for the sun!)

The Great Spirit can be found at the centre of all living things – including you. Often we humans have a tendency to see only ourselves at the centre of our universe, which is one of the reasons why we feel separated.

Like the circle, you have only one centre. This is your still point, where you can find and merge with your co-creator. You can find this timeless point through your breath, meditation, and other energy work. Spending most of your time in your heart, rather than your head, will keep you close to it.

At every heartbeat, there is one tiny moment of time when your heart is neither expanding nor contracting – when you are infinite and all that you are is seen and vibrating clearly to the entire universe. This is the point to go to when you wish to 'centre yourself' and draw upon your power.

Now, place yourself in the circle – draw another dot representing you.

Next, make a dot in your circle of life for the animals, trees, plants, rocks, flowers and all living things that surround you.

Where did you place yourself? Where did you place the animals? The trees?

You'll spot that all the living things revolve around the centre, the creator. This also reveals that all things are equal. You are no greater or lesser than the animals and flowers around you. They have a life cycle just as you do.

Now draw a straight and direct line from each individual dot to the centre dot. What do you notice?

I expect you will see that every living thing on our planet has a direct connection to the centre of the circle of life and to spirit. You can also see that each dot does not depend on something else to connect it. Only you can connect yourself to the centre. The tree in your garden, your dog, and your cat, just like you, have the same direct connection to the creator and have equal access to source – this is why cats are Zen masters!

One gift Nature has is that she is always in the still point – she has deep roots and stays strong. She radiates stillness, strength and spirit and you can use her to reinforce your direct connection to your centre.

She will help you to humble yourself when you are overwhelmed and find it difficult to appreciate the gift of life that you have. When you've had a bad day, she will gently guide you to your rightful place in the universe where you can feel belonging once again.

It is our connections within life's circle that need our attention and preservation. We need to recognise our interconnectedness with the rest of the planet and beyond if we wish to continue living in a beautiful world.

How Does Your Circle of Life Fit into the Great Mosaic?
There is an old Chinese Buddhist metaphor called Indra's Net that perfectly explores the interconnectedness of all Life.

In a faraway heavenly kingdom, ruled by the giant god Indra, hangs a large jewelled net, so very, very big, and very, very wide, that it has no beginning or end. To you and me it looks like an intricate spider's web, woven from light, and on each join, there hangs a glittering jewel, each one unique and, like the net, infinite in number. It's a magical sight to behold. From a distance these precious gems look like glittering stars, but if you zoom in closely on one of the jewels you will see that it is multifaceted, and every other jewel in the whole net is reflected in that one jewel. Each jewel reflected in that single gem also reflects all the other jewels, so the process of reflection is also itself infinite. Everything contains everything else. At the same time, each individual thing is not hindered by or confused with the other individual things.

You and I are each multifaceted jewels hanging from the vast web of life; we are not only reflections of ourselves, but we also reflect everything around us. Whatever we do to one jewel affects the entire net, as well as ourselves.

What Wild Wisdom Can You Draw from This?

Remembering your connectivity is with the whole planet and all the species here on Earth is empowering and will change your world and life for the better. By spending more time in Nature, you are going straight to the source of your nourishment; you are rolling around in the heart of life. And this 'nourished you' affects a change in me and every other being.

Your connection to the natural world supports your personal growth and the growth of your community. It increases your feelings of empathy, compassion and understanding, cares for the Earth, and encourages you to be more mindful of how your actions influence other species. It affirms your sense of belonging to something greater and more permanent than you.

This interconnectedness and interdependency is how Nature keeps us safe and it's how she balances, recycles, repairs, reconciles and neutralises damage without loss of integrity or energy. It's how we are kept strong. It's also why we innately strive for balance and how we can repair, neutralise and reconcile – by feeling, remembering, and knowing our connection to the whole.

Reinforcing Your Connections

Pretty Patterns Are Paramount

Nature creates patterns for us to find beauty in and we are asked to respond by painting our own beautiful pattern, and just like the ripple effect in water, our beautiful pattern adds to Nature's beautiful pattern and so she expands and grows as we do.

When we feel separate from the whole we cannot use our eagle-eye vision – we don't see our individual beauty or the beauty that surrounds us and are unable to reflect it. We reflect what we see.

If we add an untruthful, inauthentic pattern to the whole it will distort it, knocking it out of balance and symmetry. Ultimately, life gets ugly! We see this ugly pattern and respond by creating more ugliness – child molestation, slaughter of humans, war, greed. Need I go on? We recognise unnatural ugliness when we see it. Ugly patterns leave us feeling separate and weaken our connection to life. We are Nature and are wired to contribute to the whole – to be and add to the beautiful artwork that is this planet.

Ugly Patterns Accumulate Negative Energy

One of my clients had accumulated such a vast store of heavy dark energy with his repeated pattern of violence, prison, and drugs that his lungs collapsed and his breathing was severely restricted.

Breathing secures our jewel's position on the glittering net, and he had almost severed himself from his vital life source. The doctors gave him little hope but, intuitively, he knew he could heal himself. I assisted him in neutralising this antagonistic energy with my Alchemy healing system and working with angelic guides.

When he returned home from his week spent on the retreat in India, an X-ray showed that his lungs were healed. He was then faced with a choice of creating a new pattern or repeating the old. He decided to turn his life around and create a new pattern. This one choice caused a ripple effect of beauty; he has written a book to inspire others stuck in similar perpetuating patterns, he has trained as a reiki healer and is supporting healing in others, and he is giving back to his local community by caring for autistic adults.

What Wild Wisdom Can You Draw from This?

We don't necessarily need to make such extreme changes to our whole pattern to make a positive difference. One simple act of kindness will send positive ripples across the infinite net, touching every jewel, every person and thing in existence.

This ripple effect is why your beliefs, choices and actions and your energy trail are so important; not only do they create your life, they also impact on 'the whole'. You matter.

I believe our planet is going through an Alchemy Moment of its own right now. Alongside the distress caused by terrorism and environmental destruction, there is a huge shift in pattern and shape happening, causing uncertainty and turmoil throughout our world. On the upside this is encouraging us to seek alignment, to recognise that we have become disconnected from Nature, and to reclaim our vital power source.

Nature the Artist

What Can Nature Teach the Life Artist?

As I said in the previous chapter, often the biggest barrier to our creations is doubting that we can create something from nothing. In this section, we will observe how Nature creates healthy, lasting creations and what we can learn from her processes.

Let's get started:

Find an Environment Where You Can Flourish

To create something from nothing we need the best environment for it to grow. One of the greatest things Nature taught me was to invest in the power of my environment; it has a tremendous impact on our lives and everything we create.

For years, I had been composing settings in the theatre and classroom to optimise desired outcomes. Wearing my blinkers at the time, I didn't apply this to myself until I intuitively jumped onto a plane and flew off to sunny lands. It was then I truly felt the impact that environments have on us, our lives and all we create.

Nature teaches you that for any creative endeavour you need to have the right starting conditions for your creation to unfold. Remember the infinite bar where you picked up potential? Well, now you've 'sparked' you'll need to take potential to a suitable environment – one that is able to feed, nurture and hold it while your creation grows.

Have you ever tried starting a diet when you have a cupboard full of biscuits? It's not very successful! To manifest anything, we have to check the starting conditions are able to support what we desire in the given environment. That does not mean we can't create it. It just means we may also have to change our environmental conditions – in this case, bring in some delicious, healthy snacks and bin the biscuits.

What Wild Wisdom Can You Draw from This?

When you experience difficulty creating your desires, take a look at the environment and conditions you are choosing. If you seem to be repeating the same old toxic relationships or unfulfilling jobs ask yourself, "What do I need to flourish?" Sometimes only a few small changes will be needed for your seedling to thrive. Sometimes you may have to construct an artificial environment. A Keralan Pineapple won't grow naturally in Scotland, but you can place it in a greenhouse and recreate tropical conditions.

Sometimes you will need to take action and find a completely new environment in which to thrive – like leaving your toxic relationship or job. Sometimes a plant will defy all logic and grow despite its terrible conditions. As a Life Artist, only you can decide the best conditions for your creations. If you get stuck, let your soul's joy guide you.

Where Do You Flourish?

Although I live in the UK, I spend around four months of my year in India, because at the moment, these are the conditions supporting me to grow and flourish. I love my friends, my family and my beautiful home in Devon – comfortable and secure with a soft bed! I also love the challenge, vibrant energy and the thrill of adventure in India. I find that the perfect blend of these contradictory environments provides me with a vast amount of creative opportunity that continues to defy and expand my perception. To discover and co-create these conditions for myself I listened to the nudges from my soul and used shamanic journeying; I received guidance from spirit and followed it one step at a time. Then my work, relationships and finances naturally aligned to make this happen and support my growth.

This doesn't mean I don't have limitations – the financial predator has stalked me quite a few times! Yet, it is limitation that shapes the form our creative energy takes. It is vital for us to recognise this because it keeps us focused on our vision when things become uncomfortable.

Creating the right conditions is often challenging. When I first started to create this lifestyle, I had to accept necessary limitation for it to manifest. This was scary, heart-wrenching and exhilarating all at the same time, and it took a difficult and mighty leap of faith on my part.

I had to leave my secure job and accept I would have no stable income; I had to rent out my home, part with my beloved cats, stop performing with the band, and limit my other activities for a time, so that my chosen lifestyle could become a reality.

I must also remember that everything has a cycle and that this one won't last forever. One day these conditions won't be right for me to continue flourishing, and my life will change yet again. This leads me nicely on to the next important point that Nature can teach us.

Surrender and Uncertainty

There is an unpredictability to all creative processes; this is what makes it both exciting and nerve-wracking. As a Life Artist, Nature can teach you how to live with unpredictability, when to surrender and when to move forward.

One of our biggest problems as human beings is learning and relearning our place within life's natural cycle. When we do, we suffer and crave less. Having said that, it's not easy. We are emotional and sensitive beings, investing heart and soul into life.

It is very easy to become attached to our creations. This is why we happily forget the natural laws of surrender and uncertainty. But, in doing so, we stop trusting in the process of life. In order for change and transformation to take place, a space must be created – the old must die and transform into something new.

What Wild Wisdom Can You Draw from This?

Staying attached to your creations causes your energy to stagnate and creates physical and emotional imbalances in your body. Co-creating with spirit will keep your trust strong and when you make mistakes – which you will sometimes – remember to wrap up warm in the cloak of kindness and forgive yourself.

As we discovered earlier, the life of all things is cyclical. If you learn to recognise the process – when your creation is growing, when it is at its peak, when it is in a process of decay, or when it has died – life transitions become easier to cope with and you can begin to surrender.

Beware of sitting in the reclining chair of decay to keep your beloved creations alive. You can get so comfortable there that you stop growing wildly. It causes you to latch on to the past, live in regret, and lose your vision; it drains your vital energy, making you miserable. Things rot in decay – so you end up rotting. Like putting an old, sick dog to sleep, it's kinder and healthier to let it go.

How do we know if we are in decay?
Ask yourself: "Am I Resisting Change?"

If you resist change you will start to sacrifice yourself. I totally misunderstood the idea of sacrifice when my relationship was in decay. The icing on the cake was when my partner got ill with depression and I tipped into complete denial. I felt I should give up all of my needs for the sake of the relationship; that was the 'correct' thing to do.

Many of us give up on our needs unwittingly to be 'nice', 'good', or 'kind', or because we don't want to face the pain. We do it for our children, partner or work. If you do this often, have a good look to see if it serves you in some way. Are you deriving your self-worth from self-sacrifice? Are you avoiding feeling pain or dealing with change?

Sacrificing ourselves keeps us small and it creates co-dependency and denial, alongside an unfulfilled existence. In the opposite vein, some people believe they shouldn't give of themselves at all, breeding selfishness and conceit.

How do you find a happy balance? How can you give yourself
without losing yourself?

Healthy Sacrifice

One great way to understand the process of surrender is with the analogy of a tree. The seed sacrifices itself so that the tree can be born and provide fruit. Those fruits contain hundreds of new seeds and, so, the cycle of life goes on. This is natural sacrifice and the process and impermanence of life.

Here you can find a balanced natural way as a guide. The seed's purpose is to sacrifice itself for the growth of the tree and by fulfilling its purpose it gives life. It simultaneously gives back to the Earth and reaches its full potential by doing so.

Ask yourself this question: "Is my sacrifice beneficial? Can I still fulfil my purpose and bear fruit?"

At times, Nature seems cruel and can provide us with tough choices that bring about painful change. When you are faced with these types of choices it's helpful to remember that you ought to also be able to naturally fulfil your purpose, give back to the Earth and reach your full potential while upholding them. If the sacrifice knocks you out of alignment, stops you from growing and being true to yourself, it's not healthy or beneficial. It's not natural for your soul and will leave you feeling dispirited.

What Wild Wisdom Can You Draw from This?

Trust the process.

Our fear of change brings us more anguish than change itself. Change is naturally regulated in Nature; we cannot change into something we are not supposed to, which is why we must relinquish control and trust the growth lessons life is offering us.

When you let nature into your heart, you can cope with change in a more effective way. You can safely let go and trust in the natural cycle of life. Holding on to something that naturally needs to change interferes with Nature's process. If the tree held on to the seed, the seed wouldn't be able to fulfil its purpose and, consequently, there would be no more trees. If you move with the cyclical flow, Nature will heal your wounds. By immersing yourself in her and trusting in your own magnificent power, she will keep you growing in the right direction.

Create from Your Natural Light

Nature shines her Sun for things to grow and she brings colour to our world with light. She is an expert light worker, and we are blessed with the ability to be one too.

We are visual creatures; we predominantly perceive the world through light, and just like the artist, we work with light daily. Our 'sun' is regulated by our perception; we are able to experience the world by literally bringing to life what we focus upon. Nature has given us the ability to construct our worlds and she trusts us to contribute to the bigger picture, to add to the beauty of the whole planet.

Your connection to your sun, just like Nature's connection to the Sun, is the most critical you have. It is through natural sunlight that Nature emits the energy that brings life to all things. This is why it is essential to understand the quality of the energy you emit and how you can influence it. We will explore this in the next chapter.

Artificial light emits energy, but not in the same quantity or quality as sunlight – and it also requires energy to light it and so uses more of it. Natural sunlight effortlessly allows all living things to grow fully. The same applies to us as creators. When you shine 'your original', authentic and natural sun – rather than an artificial, unnatural version – and you use that energy to create with, then your art and your life will flourish.

What Wild Wisdom Can You Draw from This?

Remember it takes much more of your energy to light up the artificial you. This is why the 'wild' original you matters so much. By being authentic and naturally you, you are healthy and thriving. You can contribute your art to the beautiful mosaic and fulfil your purpose easily.

Just like the seed, you contain all the instructions necessary to sprout to life as the natural you, but you must first grow deep and healthy roots. You also need an environment that is full of the right nutrients to sustain you. When you buy a packet of dry seeds the seeds are inactive or dormant and all it takes to wake them up is a bit of water. Your connection to spirit is your watering can, supporting your roots to grow strong. Whenever you feel inactive or dormant immerse yourself in spirit; take a walk with Nature, meditate, dance, ask for guidance. In essence, communicate.

An important element to remember when we are eager for our authentic creations to grow is timing. If a seedling sprouts too soon, it will wilt and die prematurely. We must nourish our creations until they are ready, trust in perfect timing, and practise patience.

Contour Your Shadows To Illuminate Your Light

Creating from our natural light doesn't mean we deny our shadow self. On the contrary, like all artists, it is essential we look at and blend both light and shadow to create striking and authentic art. After all, light forms everything we see, bringing information to us about our environment. Blocked light forms shadows; when light shines onto an object, and the object blocks the light, the light will fall sideways of the object and create a shadow.

It's the same for us; our shadows exist because there is no direct light shining on them, and so, we have very little information about them. They only stay shadows because we choose not to look at them – we block the light. Carl Jung defined the shadow as the unknown 'dark side' of our psyche. It consists of our unexpressed parts – both helpful and harmful.

We all have a shadow side. The Shadow is what you perceive as dark and weak about yourself, and therefore needing to be hidden and denied. Our shadows contain our deepest desires, instincts and drives; we sense their power and fear their expression, afraid that they make us unacceptable to society and ourselves. Integrating our cruelty, anger, selfishness and shame, as well as our kindness, compassion and empathy, leads us to balance and wholeness.

Even spirituality can create a shadow side! You see it arise in the New Age and self-development circles where there is a great deal of emphasis on 'staying positive' no matter what, which leads to spiritual bypassing. Spiritual bypassing is where the person uses spiritual practices and beliefs to avoid dealing with their dark and painful parts, and this disconnects them from their feelings, shields them from the truth and stops them recognising their true nature. When this happens, they aren't able to see all of their authentic power, so they start drawing on artificial light to create from, which is exhausting because it consumes more of their energy.

The creative energies of the shadow are powerful. If we continue to deny their existence, they express themselves in unexpected ways; they distort our perception and can sabotage our relationships, overwhelm our spirit, and keep us from fulfilling our dreams. These rejected, denied, feared shadow parts of yourself contain precious nectar for your creations when you integrate them and accept them as part of you.

What Wild Wisdom Can You Draw from This?

Don't become the shadow of your shadows.

To be authentic it's vital to shine a light on our unknown, unexpressed parts, to see, accept and transform the shadows we dance with.

You can recognise your shadow by 'shedding some light on it'. Become self-aware and consciously look for it, learn from it and grow from it. Explore how it is shaping your life and the images you see.

You will get an opportunity to transform and harness the power of your shadows in Part Two of the book. This will enable

The Art of You

you to explore them, integrate them and use their wisdom to spark your creations.

How To Revive Your Relationship with Nature

Try these 10 ways to revive your relationship with Nature
The best way to revive your relationship with Nature is to physically spend time with her. The following exercise offers you a variety of ways to so this.

Take a Dose of Daily Wildness
Every relationship needs a little va-va-voom! If your relationship with Nature is in need of a spark, then it's time to sample her wildness. Make time to discover your own studio space and go there daily. This could be in your garden, in the local woods or down by the riverside. Make this your go-to wild space for nourishment, nurture and abundant inspiration.

Sacred Bonding
Take a walk with friends and notice how Nature helps to create deep bonds between you. Or better still, explore the sacred through Nature together with your friends by holding a ceremony to honour her and watch how altruism, trust and generosity are increased amongst the group.

Gaze at Nature's Art
Remember the eyes are the windows to the soul. If you need a dose of Nature's medicine, but don't have time to take a trip out, try to move to a spot where you can look at her – even for five minutes. Simply looking out the window and gazing at the sky has significant and measurable effects on our physical, mental, emotional and spiritual health. When you really look at Nature and allow her to reciprocate, you will feel as though you've been hugged; your sense of well-being will increase. She induces

feelings of peace and calmness and regulates your emotions. Life's problems seem smaller: you become calmer and more equipped to deal with them.

Take a Forest Bath

We have all experienced the relaxing power of a sun bath. In Japan, they practise Shinrin-yoku which translates enchantingly as 'forest bathing' – literally luxuriating and soaking in Nature's goodness. Spend 15 minutes a day walking in Nature and absorbing the forest's medicine. It can improve your physical, mental and emotional state by decreasing feelings of anger, reducing blood pressure, improving your attention, and help you to deeply relax.

Let Nature Nurse You

Create a healing space in your garden. If you don't have one, choose a special outdoor place to go to where you feel safe. Sit quietly and let Nature still you. Breathe quietly and ask her to heal you. Do you feel like walking? Sitting? Swimming? Notice your intuitive response and act on it.

Move Closer To Her

A study in Tokyo came to the conclusion that living near natural spaces is related to a long life. It discovered that people living in areas with green spaces within walking distance made them live longer, independent of their age, sex or socio-economic status. If moving house isn't an option for you right now, you could create a natural space in your home with plants.

Get Sporty Together

Just being outdoors increases your vitality and the 'feel-good' factor. Surrounding yourself in natural settings almost instantly increases your energy. Try wild swimming in your local river, doing yoga on the beach at sunrise, or exercising outdoors rather than in a gym. This not only brings the usual benefits of exercise but will also significantly clear and align your energy.

Receive Her
Let Nature see you. When I was a little girl I used to walk across the fields to a favourite tree and sing to it. We instinctively know how to receive Nature and relate to her. Do what you did as a child – find a large tree and talk to it, or jump in the river with your clothes on! Allow her to explore you and feel your joy rise and the creative ideas come flooding in.

Let Nature Reflect Your Magnificence
Nature stimulates transcendence, allowing you to feel your divine presence. Go to her when you're feeling separate from the world and nothing is going as planned. Journey through her and absorb the feelings of timelessness and union. She will help you to overcome the limits of daily life. She feels like a friendly familiar space where you can recapture a sense of belonging and feel in the flow.

Play Footsie with Her
Walking barefoot on the Earth or 'earthing' will develop your senses and intuition and even help you to sleep! Head into your garden, or even better into a wild space, and walk barefoot on the earth. If you have trouble sleeping, try to do this under the moonlight before you go to bed. You will feel a connection growing to the Earth and its magnetic field. It will flood your body with negative ions, your awareness will grow and you will feel the pleasure of belonging as the chi is stimulated from your feet upwards. I spend three months a year virtually barefoot, walking on sand and earth, and it's undeniably a powerful energy balancer.

Snippets of Wisdom

The cosmos, Nature and humanity exist as one.

If I draw a potential energy line connecting all three I get the polarity of two worlds – day and night, up and down.

To stay balanced I must walk with one foot in each world. Nature gives me this ability and connection.

I can look to Nature for guidance on how to balance the polarity of life. The closer I am to her, the more potential energy I have. She is my Living Bridge to source.

Chapter 4

Energy As Quality

Let's paint a picture....

It's Your Choice

Create life. Create breath. Create relaxation. Create awareness. Create wide-awake potential with honouring limitation. Create stillness of lake, wildness of ocean, patience, fire, energy. Create joyful song and free-flowing dance. Create power. Create the path of the sacred warrior. Create the wisdom of your ancestors, create community, healing and illumination. Create a beautiful planet. Create the unfolding moment. Create fertile relationships. Create forgiveness, compassion, courage and kindness. Create the laughter of the clown, the passion of the goddess. Create meaning. Create action with impeccability and integrity. Create trust with acceptance and discernment. Create respect with support and self-reliance. Create flourishing dreams vibrating on four winds. Create oneness and belonging. Create gratitude, humility and resilience. Create the open-hearted warmth of wonder. Create hope. Create multi-orgasmic originality, springing from shadows, soaring with light. Create your gifts. Create love. Create a body-feeling, mind-healing, soul-uniting, spirit-expanding higher state of consciousness.

Create life.

You cut the pattern of the universe with your choice.

It's your time to awaken your magnificent natural power source, a creative well of highly-tuned consciousness. Make a difference to your planet, hold space for a loving society, embrace the pleasure and the joy of connectedness.

Starving for Connection

Can You Feel It?

Michael Jackson asks us if we can feel 'It', John Travolta strutted 'It' with disco, Maya Angelou crafted 'It' with her poetic tongue, Aretha Franklin literally sang 'It' out of her heart.

There are many ways to tune into 'It'. When we meditate, we can tune into 'It'; when we dance, we can tune into 'It'; when we walk, we can tune into 'It'.

We love fiercely when we feel 'It', and crave 'It' when we don't. Without 'It' we are a lonely, dissatisfied, disconnected and disenchanted society, who will consume anything to fill 'Its' void.

What Is 'It'?

Is 'It' energy? Yes. Chi? Yes. Life force? Yes. Cosmic mystery? Yes! Semantics can become a distraction away from 'It', but I'll try to define 'It':

'It' is a vibrational connection where all that we are is reflected, shared and experienced – a blissful merging of spirit and humanity, a knowing that we are all one and that we belong. Our state of consciousness is expanded, higher than the one we regularly tune into and live daily; we feel seen, reassured, embraced and loved – we are light.

But 'It' doesn't last long... and here lies the problem:

How Do You Fill the Void of Disconnection?

In today's society the first thing we do to fill the void is Google 'It'! Armed with our smartphones we enter into a cycle of striving; wearing our blinkers we don't recognise that having more doesn't make us feel 'It', getting thinner doesn't make us feel 'It', the job promotion doesn't make us feel 'It'. But still we believe these are the things we need.

"If only... I could have more money, be size 10 not 14, buy

a Mercedes rather than a BMW, win the lottery, get pregnant, write another book... Then I can experience 'It' constantly."

While there is nothing essentially wrong with desiring these things, 'It' cannot be found within them. Too much striving keeps us milling around in a lower consciousness and our sense of dissatisfaction increases alongside our blinkers.

There is a way to receive expanded vision, rising consciousness, reclaim our sense of 'all that we are' and stay connected to 'It'. We can learn to work with 'It' and create high quality energy, which will open a fulfilling communion with all life. But, this does require discipline and, just like baking fresh bread, we have to put the work in daily.

The Creative Process

Play your shining part on this Earth; care for her by igniting your energy, expanding your vision and expressing your art with heart.

Energy Is the Life Artist's Material

Have you ever stopped to wonder what you are creating your life with?

All artists must become intimate and skilled with the materials they use to produce authentic, high quality works of art and we are no exception.

As a Life Artist, you will soon come to understand that the one essential ingredient you need for your creations is energy. Understanding how this material works, and how you can relate to and influence it, is vital for a fulfilling, harmonious life.

Can you smell the inspiration rustling through the winds? We have everything we need, our master – Nature – has given us an abundant studio space to work in and willingly imparts her wisdom. Let's get stuck in!

The Preparation Stage

Firstly, let's get creative with the material we have to play with and understand how to work with it.

Preparation is the first stage of the creative process. It's a time to immerse yourself fully, dive deeply and explore many areas of energy, revisiting what you know, gathering fresh ideas, learning lessons and adding them all to your creative cauldron.

Revisiting what we know: Let's remember your starting point is with your authentic energy. Nature has taught us that she uses the currency of energy as her material to drive life and that to create with artificial light consumes much more of our energy and produces lower quality creations.

Nature is nourished by natural sunlight and releases the energy that brings life to all things. You create in the same way.

Let's stop and ponder that for a moment... Your authentic nature is your sun and if you create from that source you will have an amplified quantity and quality of energy nourishing your creations. That sounds great but how do you know what is naturally you and what is artificial?

As a society, we have lost our connection to Mother Earth; it has become perfectly normal to cover over what seems too 'natural' and does not fit with the status quo. In our desperate attempts to feel accepted, we hide our true selves. We eagerly cover our natural body, becoming obsessed with diets, deodorants, clothing and hair removal. When did it become 'unnatural' for a woman to have hair on her legs?

Natural ageing has become an embarrassment; we shamefully banish our years of wisdom and laughter with Botox. We spend our lives focused on accumulating money and define ourselves according to our earning potential. We even wear sunglasses indoors to prevent our vulnerable nature from shining through.

It has become normal to be artificial. It's no wonder we feel bewildered when we look for our authentic selves – we've lost sight of what is meaningfully us.

Alan Watts once said: "We are the eyes of the cosmos." If we are the eyes of the awe-inspiring, magnificent cosmos why do we fear being seen? Are we fearful to see what we have become? Or have we forgotten what we are?

'Who am I?' – A Meditation to discover the authentic you

To know what is authentically you and what is not, you can take a journey to the heart of your ancient forest and search for your Mother Tree – she holds the wisdom you seek.

Let's pause for a moment... take a quiet breath and visualise together:

Imagine the green centre of your heart chakra vibrating as the blood is pumped through with each breath you take. Allow the colour to become an intense emerald green. Do this for a few minutes or as long as you need to build the vibrant green colour in your mind's eye.

Next, hold the intent to meet your Mother Tree: Allow time for her celestial branches to open; hear her dangling wishes whispering in your winds; open your heart and receive her...

The Mother Tree of your heart's forest holds ancient wisdom and connects your entire forest together acting as a hub, feeding and uniting all that dwells in the forest. Once she has appeared to you, enter her roots and offer your wish *"to be shown all that you are"* on the altar that lies ahead.

Allow her whispers of wisdom to embrace you, rest in her a while and sip meaning from her medicine cup.

Go deeper and climb down the winding staircase into the Earth's crystal core. Stand on the crystal and allow the vibrating energy to flow upwards through your feet, rising until it spills over the top of your crown chakra. Notice the crystal vibrations bringing you clarity as you remember *'all that you are'*. Thank your Mother Tree for her life-sustaining wisdom.

Bask in the feeling and sense of *'all that you are'*.

Slowly bring yourself back to the present moment.

With the energy of 'all that you are' flowing through you, the next question to ask yourself is, *"Who do I think I am?"* It's your answer to this question that will determine how you express *'all that you are'* in your daily life.

You cannot alter the energy of *'all that you are'*, you can only see and experience more of it by expanding your consciousness. But, you do have a choice over *'who you think you are'* and it can be changed. In fact, it alters momentarily depending on how fragile or confident you feel. This can become a problem because the energy relationship between *'all that you are'* and *'who you think you are'* must be harmonious for you to recognise your authentic gifts and express them.

One good way of balancing these energies is by adding the energy of humility into the mix. Humility will teach you to accept all of you, and think of yourself less. I do this by regularly asking the question, *"How can I serve?"*

When your attention is on how you can serve, it begins to align the energy of *'who you think you are'* with the energy of *'all that you are'*, directing them to support you to express your true nature in whatever it is you wish to do. When you do this regularly you become true to yourself.

Your Authentic light activates a natural spring of amplified and high quality energy. As a Life Artist, this is a great starting point – this means you have access to free, high quality material to work with – and all you need to receive this is to be true to yourself.

What Happens If You Are Untrue To Yourself?

Your authentic light offers you all the colours of the rainbow to work with. When you are untrue to yourself your colours become weaker. You are essentially blending imbalanced energy and this turns the palette muddy. This taints your creations and takes extra effort to clean it up. To keep your rainbow brilliant and clean, create from your authentic light.

When we are untrue to ourselves it also has an impact on our bodies – we become weaker spiritually, emotionally, and physically.

The Impact of Truth on Your Body

Energy flows through our bodies in specific patterns and when one energy pattern is exposed to other energy patterns such as words, thoughts, colours, music, people, food, plants, crystals – well, absolutely anything – it responds. This response creates reactions in our body.

One of the exercises I use in my workshops to demonstrate the body's response to energy is a Kinesiology muscle test. I'll ask Rosie to hold her arm out and say her real name out loud, as I simultaneously apply gentle pressure to her hand. The molecules in her body respond and her arm stays strong.

I then repeat the procedure but ask Rosie this time to tell me an untruth – that her name is John or Julie for example. Rosie holds out her arm and says her name is Julie, while I apply the same amount of gentle pressure as previously. This time her arm weakens and drops.

People are often amazed at this little test because there is nothing they can do to stop the weakness, no matter how much resistance they put up…

I also repeat the same process with two bits of paper. One piece has the words *I love you* written on it and the other has *I hate you*. I give Rosie one of the two pieces of paper to hold in her hand, and ask her to hold her arm out as before. This time her arm is extremely weak. I lay that piece of paper down in front of her without opening it.

I repeat the process with the other piece of paper and her arm is extremely strong. As you probably guessed, her muscles responded with weakness to the paper with *I hate you* written on it and with strength to *I love you*. Rosie had no idea what was written on either piece of paper.

Dr David Hawkins developed an entire Scale of Consciousness based on this muscle testing technique and discovered that there is a critical point (200 being the level of courage on his scale) where everything that calibrates below this point makes the body go weak and represents the absence of 'truth'. Everything above 200 makes the body become strong and represents the presence of truth.

As you can see, living your truth matters. It is how you can strengthen your physical, emotional and spiritual body as well as transcend consciousness.

Also, the more you create with truth, the more truth you will accumulate. It's a win-win cycle of flow which empowers you by increasing the resonance of your being.

There's an expression in the acting community that is drummed into all actors – "find your light". It means that if you're in the dark on stage, step into the light so you can be seen. If you also remember this simple tip before starting your creative endeavours, you too can create your truth and leave a trail of beauty behind you.

Gathering Ideas and Understanding Your Material

Our united purpose is to express our 'original truth' and energy is what we use to do this. How we do it is unique for each of us and depends on the choices we make.

You can choose how you use energy, yet most of us don't realise this and don't know the choices available to us.

The following section will dig a little deeper and give you a better understanding to make informed choices to create your beautiful life.

What Is Energy?

What is this invisible power that we create our lives from? I remember having to explain this question to a bunch of sweaty boys who had just come off the football pitch. They were attending my drama class. I asked one boy to project the energy of his character and he cunningly answered: "I can't, Miss. I don't have any left – I've just played a match!" I explained that he was talking about his physical energy and he had other types of energies he could use.

Depending on whether we're actors, footballers, scientists or shamans, we will answer this question from a different perspective. I am answering this question from the Shamanic perspective firstly, because my work, experience and heart have led me here and, secondly, because it is all encompassing.

Shamanism believes that everything has a spirit, everything is energy, everything is vibration and everything is connected. Basically, our ever-evolving star-studded mosaic is one beautiful vibrating spirit, and all things contribute and shape it with their own vibrational frequency.

Although the scientist would phrase this quite differently, there is vast evidence in recent years to suggest that the majority of the science community essentially now agrees with this view.

Just like your circle of life on Earth that you explored in the previous chapter, the Great Spirit is also at the centre of our beautiful patterned mosaic. Everything that is known, and unknown, contains the essence of Spirit – the planets, stars, rivers, you, your cat! We are living in an interconnected and interdependent universe with energy as the source of all creative life.

Pattern: The Foundation of Creation

The Great Spirit is a Life Artist and uses the pencil of repetitive vibration to draw life from energy. It is constantly sketching, pattern after pattern, repeating connections and making new ones. You and your great mosaic are made up of pattern and so is your material world.

You have inherited this gift of pattern – it's the starting point for all your creations. Your vibrational frequency creates your personal energy patterns. This is why the quality of your energy is crucial because it is used to sketch out your reality; you then colour it in with your memories, thoughts and feelings in order to experience it.

Your daily habits may be simple patterns of behaviour but they are also much more than everyday routines. They hold your patterns of reality in place and are extremely important in shaping your life.

For example, making daily meditation a habit can stimulate the energy of compassion, kindness and love, creating a higher vibrational pattern and bringing more light into your life. The habit of criticising yourself and others will produce a lower, darker vibrational pattern. Some habits will raise your vibe, others will not. You will have a chance to explore your patterns in a practical way in Part Two.

Exploring Your Energy Systems

There are two powerful and creative energy systems that are gold-dust for the Life Artist to grasp. This is because they give our lives form and shape – and we are all about creating form and shape. The first of these is the Chakra system and the second is Morphogenic Fields. With an understanding of the creative uses of these tools, you will be able to make magic!

The Chakra System – Yee Haw!

I expect you have come across the chakra system – you definitely worked with your chakras when you opened your heart and we did the Mother Tree visualisation together earlier in the chapter. So, this is a flying visit to refresh us before we explore the process of creation through the chakras.

The chakra system is ancient. We know that it was first written about in the Vedas. These ancient holy texts originate from my second home of India – which happens to be where I'm writing these words, absorbing her wisdom and consciousness. There are seven major chakras that are most commonly referred to, but we actually have many more. For example, I will initiate and open the hand chakras when I give a reiki healing attunement.

For now, let's focus on the Magnificent Seven – Western movie pun intended! Their job is to keep your inner world and outer world balanced and flowing freely. The chakra system acts like a bridge between your spirit, body and mind. It's your rainbow palette of galloping cowgirls herding your consciousness through your body, each one with its own territory to protect.

You are the Sheriff with the job of keeping all these seven chakras singing in harmony. Yours is an important job because these seven energy centres organise the way you receive, assimilate and transmit energy. If there's conflict and a shoot-out, barricades go up, areas become blocked and there's a lot of crazy spinning. The singing stops and you become weak or ill – physically, mentally and spiritually.

This imbalance can happen if you favour one chakra and overuse it, or restrict and ignore an area allowing it to become dim, dirty or clogged. One way to ensure harmony reigns is to ride into town regularly to visit each chakra, attend to issues and find solutions that generate balance.

Chakra Energy in the Creative Process

Nature's Favourite Pattern

Let's head back to our teacher Nature for a moment, to understand the flow of our energy in creation. Nature's favourite geometric pattern, which is at the heart of all creation, is called the Torus. It's Nature's way of sustaining and creating life – it's the signature of source left in all its masterpieces. Yes, you are a masterpiece!

Its shape is like a tasty-looking doughnut filled with energy that flows inwards on top of itself and spirals down, flowing outwards and back in. This energy is continually refreshing and influencing itself, and adapts to the form it fills. You can spot it obviously in apples, tornadoes, smoke rings, our breath. It underlies all creation, including ourselves.

Our Torus pattern of energy surrounds our physical body and forms our aura. The aura contains seven layers and each layer is the 'territory' governed by each of the Magnificent Seven chakras. This is how you emit, receive and translate energy.

Aura Territory – Magnificent Seven
Etheric body – Root chakra
Emotional body – Sacral chakra
Mental body – Solar plexus
Astral body – Heart chakra
Etheric double – Throat chakra
Celestial body – Third eye
Causal body – Crown chakra

The aura is the Island that houses and protects your chakras. It plays a major part in protecting your overall health, immunity and vitality. Many things collect on its shoreline that can influence your natural presence; the electromagnetic frequencies of smartphones, Wi-Fi and computers, etheric energy and the energy of others, which can all weaken the protection of the aura and create an imbalance with your authentic energy flow.

These energies are subtle, yet appear like plastic bags on a beautiful beach; we notice their impact and feel run-down, 'out of sorts' or heavy. It's a good idea to make a regular practice of clearing the debris that washes up on your shores. You can do this by applying the energy tools at the end of the chapter.

Healing and meditation work pays attention to the chakras because they are entry points – portals to send and retrieve information from energy. You, as Sheriff, have the ability to use this information to heal yourself and create and maintain the quality of your life. You have a direct channel to source.

To grasp the understanding we need for this section, I have broken down your energy system into parts. But it's important to consciously view the aura, the chakras and the constant energy flowing through it as a whole. It's a complex, interdependent and interconnected system, ever evolving and changing. As a whole it creates your presence in the universe and it offers you a chance to expand your presence on the planet and beyond.

The Natural Flow of Creation

As we know, nature's doughnut-shaped Torus has an upward and downward energy flow and so do we. It's the ebb and flow of life – our cycle. Understanding how we use both the liberating and manifesting energy flow in the creative process is a skill the Life Artist can grow and benefit from.

The Liberation Flow – Up, Up and Away!

The Liberation flow is the upward energy stream. It is transcendent and liberating in quality. This flow is herded up through our root chakra and flows out through our crown chakra. It guides us to peel back our blinkers and frees us of constricting habits and identities. When we liberate ourselves, our matter transforms – we are moved beyond what we know, entering unknown realms of consciousness.

This transcendent space is where – if you play your cards right – you meet your co-creator for a divine date! It's the bar where you pick up potential, where you can catch creative ideas of inspiration and potential dreams floating around the cosmos. This energy flow creates a blissful state and we become lighter – we 'enlighten' as we remove the dimness from our vision and our hearts.

The Liberation energy is stopped or hindered when we have forgotten to 'Sheriff' ourselves properly. Our galloping cowgirls kick off and there's a shoot-out! For example, you may have a problem letting go of an abusive relationship and despite knowing you should leave, you stay in it because you fear being alone. This creates havoc throughout your energy system and blocks you from growing and moving on with your life. This causes the energy to stagnate and your life with it, leaving you feeling dull and stifled. We need to be balanced and learn from our blockages to transcend.

To access liberation, we must be willing to release, reveal and accept.

As you know, this energy is our pathway to developing greater and higher awareness. If we allow, it will transform us and release us from our physical attachments, providing infinite possibilities and potential.

The Manifesting Flow – What Goes Up Must Come Down!

The manifesting energy is highly creative. It's a downward energy spiral that pulls pure consciousness through the crown chakra to the root chakra, finally manifesting into form on the physical plane. This flow is how we live and function in the world around us. We use it all the time, but often with a potluck outcome.

The manifesting flow must be physically pulled down through the chakras and sculpted through a fine balance of creative fire, boundaries, limitation, resilience and discipline. It's like giving birth!

I am going through the process right now as I'm writing these words and it's challenging! I have consciously chosen the best conditions for myself to write and I know the limitation won't be forever. I'm putting the boundaries in place by creating regular writing slots and disciplining myself to show up – whether I feel like it or not. Those colourful cowgirls are galloping hard. Right now, it would be more painful to stop than to continue, so I have to keep going! The creative fire is intense, and the more I take creative action, the hotter the fire becomes.

If you're now holding the book in your hand, you'll know I was successful!

Finding the Wisdom in Your Creations

There is learning contained in each inspirational spark, idea or potential dream we pick up when floating about in the liberation flow. It's like a golden chest of treasure. The only way to open the chest is to manifest these inspirations and dreams on the physical plane – in your life. As you go through the process of manifestation the insight you receive from your transcendence can be reflected back to you through the creative process and the art-full life you produce.

A good example of this is my personal story. As you know I was living a dull and stagnated existence, unwilling to let it go until an Alchemy Moment swooped down and cracked me open. This forced me to unblock myself and catch the liberating current where I transcended and was handed some treasure. I travelled the world, learnt lessons, discovered my gifts and I saw that life loved me.

I knew I had received treasure, but I had no idea just how beautiful it was until I manifested it into a physical form. My creations became 'truth reflectors'. The pattern of my treasure has multiplied and evolved into many forms – healings, retreats, courses, books, relationships, businesses. This is giving me a fulfilling life. But, more importantly, each art form I create is teaching me and reflecting truths that enable me to keep growing and see more of 'all that I am'.

When you create art, your truth is reflected back in a similar way to a holograph. The essence of your light is recorded and beamed into a new form so that you can see more of it and simultaneously help others to see theirs. They also grow and expand – we are the multifaceted jewels on Indra's Net.

The entire cycle of liberating and manifesting moves us

towards wholeness; we can uncover our truth and all that we can be in this lifetime. Understanding how to work with it brings meaning to our lives.

Habits of Creation

Let's go back to Nature again. How does she manage all her marvellous creations and never tire? Even though she has taught us to embrace the mystery of creation, she is also highly organised, has a great memory, and loves to create with repetition and habit.

The term Morphogenic Fields was coined by biologist Rupert Sheldrake whose research concluded that Nature organises and evolves through habits and memory. Everything in Nature has a collective memory – an energy field created and added to by resonance. All form has consciousness and all form creates an energy resonance within and around it. Simply put, everything has a spirit.

The Morphic Members' Club

A morphic field is like a members' club with a couple of dancing attractors outside influencing you to enter! Blue tits, birds, rivers, crystals, cultures, humanity, people who sit in armchairs – they all have one. This morphic members' club takes on a life of its own acting as a whole system that works on the premise of probability.

Many people who nestle down in their armchairs nod off to sleep. If I get influenced by the dancing attractors surrounding my armchair and join the 'armchair club' by spending a great deal of time in my armchair it's probable that I will also start nodding off. In fact, if I do make it a habit of falling asleep regularly in my armchair, this will add to the strength of the collective energy, increasing the likelihood that others will also nod off. And so, the armchair club grows! The habits of all the members past and present – behaviours, thoughts, emotions, cultures, collectives – are stored in the club's collective memory.

How Do Your Morphic Clubs Shape Your Life?

The morphic field is powerful knowledge for you to use because it's one way to shape yourself and your life and keep it growing in the direction you want.

You can tap into and use ready-made fields of consciousness to create your wish.

For example, I have caught the divine spark of inspiration and I want to become a hairstylist. What can I do? I know I must find the best environmental conditions for my creation to grow, so I 'join the club', so to speak. I take action and find a job in a salon.

My repetitive activity of turning up to work at a salon every day creates a pattern of energy that secures my entrance into the hairstylists' field of consciousness, and influences my behaviours and pattern of activity even further. Now, habits are subject to natural selection, so if my mum was already a stylist, there would be more of a probability that I would become one and that I would take to it easily as the resonance in my energy field would already be there.

After some time, I am likely to adopt the characteristics and shape of a hairstylist, take an interest in the fashion industry, develop more of a fascination for how I look, experiment with my hair, wear a lot of black, rarely have a Saturday free, develop my creativity, empathy and communication skills, frequently say the words, "Where are you going on holidays this year?" I will surround myself with hairstylist friends, all resonating a similar vibe, and I may even date a hair stylist.

Dating someone of the same profession happens a great deal in the world of education because teachers' holidays and heavy workload schedules shape their lives intensely. So, unfortunately, do breakdowns.

Illness due to stress is a strong habit of the morphic field of teachers and it's growing. It was common amongst many of my work colleagues over my 15 years in the profession. I worked in the hair industry for around ten years, and in that time, I never heard of any hairstylist signed off long-term sick with stress or depression. Morphic fields have an incredible influence in shaping our lives.

What Morphic clubs do you belong to?

Are We Morphic Members for Life?

Once we have entered a morphic field and have built up a strong resonance with it, it's difficult to leave. It influences you and you influence it. I haven't been practising as a hairstylist for many years, but I still belong to the club. I still have the skills – albeit rusty – and I now work with the industry in my new form.

I design training programmes supporting staff creativity and wellness, in both the hair and education fields, approaching them from a new angle, merging my energy, meditation and personal development work. By doing this repetitively I am slightly influencing the resonance of the fields.

If we want to change a morphic field and create a higher resonance, we need support. If thousands of people joined me in doing this or similar training, and added their resonance, it would shape the morphic fields of consciousness to include energy, wellness, and meditation work as part of a regular experience for hairstylists, teachers, and their clients and students. The more people who add their energy to a field, the stronger it becomes. This would then help to dissolve the growth of stress in education, and increase creativity throughout all fields; the benefits are infinite.

This is why people unite together to meditate for peace or hold women's groups to spread the uprising of the feminine energy. The power lies not in the physical, it lies in the energetic resonance and intent to shape a conscious, loving future.

We have been exploring morphogenic structures in societal terms to appreciate their impact on our lives. But there are fields for literally everything and this is what is so empowering.

When I attune someone to become a reiki healer, for example, their vibrational frequency is altered so they can resonate with and access the higher vibrational realm of reiki healers and masters. This is the place they can retrieve sacred wisdom and knowledge. If they adopt the habits of the field and use them – the reiki principles and symbols – and apply their learnings, they will be able to retrieve esoteric knowledge.

We are all part of one massive Morphic Mosaic. We can never leave it because we are it! It's important to remember your significance and that you do have influence over your world and mine; you can choose to have higher vibrational physical, emotional, and spiritual experiences.

Every Breath You Take… Makes a Difference

The musician Sting reflects great truth with his song, *Every Breath You Take*, every smile, action, movement, choice you make or don't make… everything… is shaping you and will reflect back to you in some form.

Absolutely everything is forming the world in which we live. You are in a constant state of creation. You have complete freedom over what you create with this powerful energetic system. Every act of kindness, loving thought, or act of community support makes a difference. So does every harmful act, ill thought or greedy notion.

You can harm or you can heal. You can go along with the status quo or you can change it. Let your soul guide your choice. The great mosaic will reflect whatever you put into it and will continue to do this at all times whether you acknowledge it or not. You have incredible power to manifest and shape your loving, conscious world.

Making Your 'Matter' Matter!

What matters to you?

We have infinite experiences available to us. There is no need for us to feel stuck or bound by our physical world because we have the power to change things.

Now you know just how much you actually matter, it's important for you to figure out what matters to you; what is it that you actually wish to experience in your lifetime?

Have a think about what really matters to you, what you care about.

Once you've decided what you care about, participating and making a difference that really matters couldn't be any easier than it is today. Put your creations out there and live a conscious life. Manifest your truth in any and every way you can and watch it go to work immediately, spreading your beauty and affecting everything you and I experience.

The Incubation Stage

Let It Brew

You have now reached the incubation stage of your creative process with energy – take some time out, let all you've explored bubble away as your subconscious and conscious mind enter into dialogue with your soul.

Why not have a brew! Sling on a Beach Boys' track and have a dance around your kitchen.

I'm off to get a massage...

While I'm writing this I'm in the middle of Panchakarma, which is a 21-day Ayurveda treatment. I've chosen to immerse myself in a 5,000-year-old, ancient morphic field; Ayurveda healing is one of nature's oldest medicine pots.

I'm going for a Kashaya Dhara. The treatment room looks as ancient as Ayurveda itself and smells like a witch's kitchen. I feel the energy emanating from the magnificent droni massage table, carved from the offering of a neem tree. As I allow it to hold me, I wonder how many people this tree continues to nourish in its new form.

There is a concoction of secret herbs bubbling in a cauldron-like pot on the old gas stove in the corner. They are being heated into a concentrate to change their state and release healing medicine. When the plant medicine is ready, it is mixed with hot water and continuously poured over me for 45 minutes by two angelic mothers.

It feels heavenly as I relax into the process; I become hotter and hotter, my body is brought to a sweat so it too can change state and release all the stresses and toxins I've been holding onto, ready to receive and absorb the herb's wisdom.

While I'm in flow, the creative floodgates open and my inspirations pour forth. I write the entire book in my mind in around 15 minutes! If only I could get up and write some of this down, I'm thinking.

While you're in your incubation stage I highly recommend you take a shower or bath. I'm a total water baby – destined to be a mermaid someday, perhaps! My creative fire loves water. If I'm stuck for inspiration I head for the bath – as did Archimedes when he first coined the term, "Eureka!"

The Illumination Stage

'The Eureka Moment'

You now enter the illumination stage of your creative process, where your creative ideas suddenly flash into existence and the obscure thing becomes clear. You uncover your message, your Eureka!

Can you feel it? Are you picking up those good vibrations?

Eureka! Raise Your Vibration!

Vibration is the way spirit moves energy through the great web of life and beyond. It's how the Cosmic Mosaic lights up and expands. All vibrations operate at high and low frequencies, within us and around us. The higher this vibrational frequency is, the closer it is to the frequency of light.

This benefits you as a Life Artist not only because you create from light, but also because the lighter your energy body, the higher you can fly. You develop a heightened perception to see space and potential. In a nutshell, when you vibrate at a higher frequency you can see more of 'all that you are' and spot your truth.

The high vibe energy you accumulate can turn on dormant centres of your mind, unclog trapped energy centres, heal pains and diseases, as well as connect you to the higher realms of collective consciousness. It's well worth cultivating!

How Can We Tell If Our Vibration Has Lowered?

It is helpful to be aware that like attracts like. When your vibration is high you expand and attract more of that type of energy. There is a beautiful sense of living in the flow. You see your opportunities and grab them. You attract inspiring people into your life and feel supported.

If your vibration has lowered it will be evident. Firstly, you will feel it. You may start to feel as though you are shrinking and are forcing life to happen. Things keep going wrong and resistance kicks in. When this happens check your perception, look for learnings, and switch to a state of gratitude and appreciation to widen your vision. It could be a signal from your co-creator that it's time to switch track and move in a new direction.

Our energy is constantly in motion and changing, our

connection to our higher energy field is always changing too. This is why one day we can feel great and, the next, down in the dumps. To ensure we maintain a balanced, healthy relationship, we must choose our thoughts, emotions and reactions consciously and wisely.

The Verification Stage

Crafting Your Message

This is the final stage of your creative exploration with energy. It's a time when you have a play around, discover what works for you, uncover the vital ingredients you need to generate quality energy, tune up your vibration and expand your presence in the world.

Throughout this creative exploration, we have discovered that we can choose to create from our essence – our authentic energy, which brings us high-quality creations. These creations are powerful; they reflect our truth and allow our sacred place in the cosmos to be revealed. We also know that if we raise our vibe we will be able to see and shine more of our essential sun. And, so, the cycle repeats, spiralling us towards being all that we can be. Eureka!

Fundamental Energy Tools

There are many practices you can choose to connect and work with energy so that you can direct it to consciously design yourself and your life. Shamanic practices, Qigong, Reiki healing, yoga, meditation, and crystal healing are just a few. All of these will act as mirrors and teachers if you embrace them as a way of life.

However, there are some simple, yet fundamental, tools that are essential for any form of energy work, and we will start by highlighting these, so that you have them tucked under your belt to work with practically in Part Two.

The four essentials to any productive energy work are awareness, intent, authentic presence and empathy. These ingredients will bring you clarity, purpose and the ability to show up and take your space in the world with a genuinely open heart. With these tools, you can unlearn the fear of your unique power and learn how to use it.

Awareness

To work with energy is to work with the feeling and to discern the subtle difference in how one energy feels in comparison to another. And the starting point for this is your awareness. Without it the observer in you is not present, which means your mind directs you, instead of you directing it. This is how many people go about their day, and it means we haven't shown up fully.

So, what can we do? We can cultivate awareness with two things:

1. Focus
2. The state of being present.

Focus is the starting point for awareness. It means knowing what is actually going on around you and where you are in the world of your story. You are able to tune into your eagle-eye vision.

Being Present

To shine your Presence you need to be Present. The state of being present is being in the here and now, in the moment, grounded in your body with your spatial awareness expanded. To do it you switch off the autopilot button, align your mind with your body and care for both. It's an important place to be because you make your choices and create in the moment. This is your point of power. In the theatre, this is called a neutral space – a space where the mind and body are balanced, unbiased and alert. It's your starting point for all of your creations.

You can cultivate 'being present' with mindfulness and meditation techniques. Your breath is your first point of call. Breathing is an instant way of changing state and finding neutral.

Mindfulness practices will help you to see your 'authentic presence' by paying attention to the moment with purpose and compassion. Creative activities that promote a neutral space, such as acting, art, dance, music or being in Nature, help to refresh and reveal your presence, bringing you a feeling of aliveness.

Intent

Intent will bring you clarity and purpose. You can use it to direct energy. You have the ability to both create with and retrieve information from energy.

Once you have full awareness with your neutral state you will be able to see with clarity and bring intent to all you do. Intention is your will, your desire, what you want to create in each moment. It is extremely powerful because it directs your energy.

Intent acts like a seed; you plant it in the fertile garden of creative consciousness and let it go by simply not thinking about it. If there is no interference your actions will naturally start to align with your intent.

Energy needs to express itself and will find a way to do this. It's driven to find a way to explore its potential; this is its nature. Energy also needs a form to be seen. If we don't give it form it will find its own, which is why we end up with messy lives sometimes. With the Life Artist's skill, you can avoid this and choose to create beautiful forms of meaning and purpose with your intent.

Presence

Your presence is the sound of your existence, the energy you exude in a space – your authentic sun. Not to be confused with 'being present'. As you know, being present is a state that leads you to see your presence, but it is not your presence. At any given moment, someone could be tapping away on their mobile as you speak to them and not be present. Presence is constant, although the amount of it that is felt or seen depends on your vibrational frequency and how present you are.

Your overall energy state in the moment is expressed as your presence and held in your aura by those galloping cowgirls! This is what you beam out to the rest of the universe and it is literally magnetic. This is how your sister or friend knows 'something's up'; they feel your presence has altered.

Each of your different energy levels – physical, mental, emotional and spiritual – has its own separate frequency which affects your overall vibration and your presence in the universe. You attract the same frequency at which you are vibrating at that moment in time.

We affect others by our presence and they affect us with theirs. Even though we all have magnetic presence, we will find we are magnetically drawn to some people's energy rather than others, which is often because we feel their authenticity and sense that they have something to reflect back or teach us.

In the theatre, it's extremely important to cultivate presence for the character to 'come alive' and be authentic on stage. It's the same for us in our daily lives – we must express our aliveness. If you are familiar with the energy of your authentic presence you will be able to notice the subtle shifts that occur to your energy and rebalance and realign yourself. You will have an opportunity to strengthen your own magnetism and presence by following the exercises in Part Two.

Empathy

Empathy means to 'feel into' something. It's the act of shape-shifting into the other, to understand it more. As Life Artists, everything is a work of art to us and we look for the beauty in it. Empathy is the way we do this. The moment we notice and project into it, we can feel the energy of anything; it transforms from an object into a work of art. The act of looking is our creative process.

Our level of empathy enables us to communicate in various degrees with everything around us, not just other humans. With a pure heart and mind, you can use empathy to commune with animals, trees, crystals, water, and it will use its own energy to respond. This is how I receive guidance for my healings and attune and work with crystals. It is a vital skill to cultivate to understand and receive information from energy.

Reflecting Your Beautiful Energy

We are the eyes of the cosmos. It's up to us to help it see its remarkable beauty. This brilliance can never be captured fully, but it can be experienced.

Being seen and heard in this communion of beauty breeds love, harmony, friendship and compassion, and it keeps high vibrational energy moving freely between all of us. If we reflect back the tremendous beauty of earth, of life, of the universe, it will be reflected back; you will feel your grandeur and preciousness.

Your creative potential and desire to create beauty will expand the whole mosaic, keeping it growing. Creating beauty allows us to become love in human form and to feel our interconnectedness.

How to Attune to a Crystal

Choose a Crystal To Work with Or Let One Choose You!

Crystals are willing spirits and make a good starting point to train yourself to work with energy. Often crystals will call out to you. Pick one that attracts you and let your intuition guide your choice. You can either work with a crystal you already own or choose one from your local crystal or online shop.

Set Your Intent:

Find a space where you will not be interrupted. Prepare yourself so that you are in a neutral state by paying attention to your breath. Set the intent to attune with your crystal. This is where your resonating energies will harmonise so that you can work and communicate with it.

Observe the Crystal:

Hold your crystal in your hand, be open and relaxed to bring your empathy forth, 'feel into' the stone and become as familiar as possible with it. Take a good look at its exterior and interior, notice the colour, texture, feel and inclusions. Inclusions are any materials trapped inside the crystal when it was formed. They can look like bubbles or lines.

Connect with the Vibration:

Now close your eyes and feel the vibration of the crystal in your hands. With your eyes still closed, feel your stone. Feel its size, shape, weight, and texture, and hold this in your mind's eye, try to memorise this. When you feel the energy, state your intent once more: that you wish to attune to the crystal and ask that the crystal works with you.

Enter the Crystal:

With your eyes still closed, imagine that you are the size of the crystal and the crystal is the size of you; then step into it, walk around and explore. Take note of any images, impressions or thoughts that come to mind while you are familiarising yourself with your crystal.

Repeat steps 1–5 every day for five days to develop resonance with your stone.

Spend Time with Your Crystal:
The next part of the attunement is to establish a connection with your crystal by spending time with it. Wear it close to your body for five days and sleep with it either in your hand or under your pillow. Keep it by you at all times, remember to take it out, look at it and 'feel into' it regularly.

Work with Your Crystal:
When you feel confident in your connection with the crystal you can begin to tune in and work with it regularly. Do this by holding the crystal in your hand and asking it what it has to teach/offer you. Again, prepare yourself with a neutral state, and 'feel into' the crystal. Be open to receive and listen to the energy of the crystal. It will speak through symbols, impressions, and feelings that come into your consciousness. The more time you spend listening and communicating with your crystal, the clearer and quicker the responses will become.

Snippets of Wisdom

When I hold an image in my mind's eye and 'feel into' that image, my understanding and connection to it increases. I can listen to its quality and hear its wisdom.

Chapter 5

Beauty As Muse

Let's paint a picture....

Beauty's Breath

A long, time ago, in a land far, far away, sat a goddess whose dress was embroidered with stars from the universe. She was an astonishingly beautiful goddess; her hair was woven from fields of flowers and her smile moved the ocean.

The great goddess stood amongst dragons of many colours. They revered her beauty and were steadfast in their adoration of her. This became disheartening for the goddess because she could not see the astonishing beauty that the dragons saw. She could only see their awestruck reactions, and the joy and pleasure they expressed.

The goddess wanted to feel the pleasure of her captivating beauty for herself.

One day the goddess had an idea and she summoned the king of the dragons.

"I am going to create a mirror so that I can see beauty," she exclaimed.

"Will you help me?"

The king of the dragons felt extremely privileged to honour the great goddess in such a way, and agreed wholeheartedly.

The goddess instructed the dragon to blow his fire into her breath on the count of three.

"One, two and three!"

The goddess sent the first breath of beauty into the universe and the dragon sent his fire. Together they blew life into all things.

Life became a mirror for the goddess and reflected her

astonishing beauty. The more she looked for beauty the more enchanting and fulfilling each day became. The goddess was happy with her newfound pleasure.

This is the final course of your divine banquet. Can you feel your roots bursting with nourished connection? There is always room for a mouth-watering dessert. Beauty is the dessert of Part One of this book. She adds the sweet taste to life. She is the definitive connection we need to make before we embark on creating our art in Part Two.

Why Beauty?

Beauty is a form of Genius – is higher, indeed, than Genius, as it needs no explanation. It is one of the great facts of the world, like sunlight, or springtime, or the reflection in the dark waters of that silver shell we call the moon. It cannot be questioned. It has divine right of sovereignty. It makes princes of those who have it.

– Oscar Wilde

I See You

Oscar Wilde hit the nail on the head when he said beauty needs no explanation; you and I can both recognise it when we see it. As humans, we inherently know the quality of beauty, we search for this archetypal energy in ourselves, each other, and our environment.

The million-dollar question is why?

We search for Beauty because it reminds us of our sacred place in the universe. Beauty is an archetype and when we recognise the image of an archetype in another form or person it also awakens that energy in us. It's Beauty's nature to illuminate any form it takes and raise it up to be seen. When awe strikes, our individual presence transcends time and space, we are momentarily exalted and merge with the 'other form' leaving us feeling validated, cherished and empowered. These are the same qualities we receive with great lovemaking. It's no coincidence that beauty has become intently associated with sex. Beauty is a pleasurable experience.

It's no wonder we will pay a fortune to have her power – to feel beauty and be beauty. This is why there is a multi-million-pound empire built in her name. Beauty is divine empathy. She 'feels into' you and offers you the gift of unity. She acts as a powerful mirror that can translate the truth of your soul and all that's required to initiate this energy is your gaze. She helps us to see that we are all part of the same beautiful mosaic.

Why a Muse?

Sing in me, Muse, sing in me, dance your creative breath into these words, and through me tell the story of that woman skilled in all ways of beauty…

As a Life Artist, we need inspiration and motivation to create our art – a divine interjection that speaks directly to our soul, keeping our authenticity and originality on track. We need a Muse!

The 'inspirational muse' that all artists seek originated from the Greek story of the Nine Muses. These wild goddesses were 'wonderwomen', saving the grace of the artist, and acting as protectors over the creative arts by generously sharing their divine gifts and spearing out oodles of inspiration to all who asked.

The muse is the territory of the feminine. Her original function was to inspire new insights and new artistic forms – with her divine breath, she protected the artist from imitation and artificiality so that they could create their unique art. The original muse took her responsibility very seriously, she was fierce and would happily poke an eye out if challenged in her role.

As a Life Artist, finding your own 'inspiring protector' is vital for your authentic expression. This chapter will enable you to summon Beauty as your Muse and engage her inspiration, power, and genius.

Why Choose Beauty as Your Muse?

To answer this question, let's first recap on what we already know:

1. Nature expresses beauty and is your teacher; she creates beauty in a variety of forms and asks you to do the same.

It's wise to honour her sacred knowledge.

2. Beauty emits a powerful energy, which has the ability to raise your vibe as soon as you gaze upon her. With beauty as your muse you can get intimate with her energy, understand how to balance it, and fill your creations with it.

3. Like energy attracts like energy. As both the artist and the art, you can set the intent to fill your creations with beauty and to become your unique expression of beauty. This cycle fills your life with enchantment. You will also become an 'experience of beauty' for others so they might be illuminated and feel validated and cherished.

4. You create from your authentic light to reveal your truth. With beauty as your muse she acts as the 'protector of your truth' as well as the 'reflector of your truth'.

5. Focusing on 'Beauty as Muse' promotes the healthy energy flow of expressing beauty to acquire it, rather than getting hung up on acquiring it.

You can see that beauty is the ultimate muse because she offers you divine sight. Divinity is like the sun. If we look directly at it, its brilliance will blind us, and that's where beauty comes in – she reflects your divine essence. She asks you to focus your gaze upon her and elevates you in the process. Your truth is supported for all to see and take pleasure in.

Choosing beauty as your muse also steers your boat towards graceful seas, inspiring connection, action and pleasurable experiences. Creating beauty in your life gives voice to your soul, expresses the sacred within you, and brings your sovereignty to the world.

Let's get started...

Evoking the Muse

Reclining on a heavily-embroidered chaise longue, stripped to her glory, Beauty will inspire you to accept your unfolding perfection and recognise the immortality of your soul. Firstly, let's get intimate with her and explore our relationship to her. Only then can we distinguish every curve, crevice and shadow that bestows her.

Dancing Beauty To Life

The presence of beauty is the result of a harmonious dance between the masculine and feminine creative energies – in other words, beauty requires balance to be seen. By this I don't mean symmetry, for beauty can emerge from inconsistency. I mean the perfect blend of masculine and feminine creative energy for the form it takes.

We have all seen the Chinese Yin and Yang symbol where two opposites coexist in harmony and are able to transmute into each other; balancing these two energies within us, our planet, and the universe, leads to spiritual transcendence, creative growth and a beautiful world. This balance is the dance of our existence, which we are all accountable for.

All of us have a unique expression of both masculine (activating) and feminine (receptive) creative energy. They work as a whole to regulate everything you and I create from a mundane thought to the creation of the universe. If you want to create beauty they must be dancing in sync with one another.

What Causes Disharmony?

If we see these creative energies as separate and distinct from each other, giving precedence to one over the other, life's creative dance loses its beauty. They move out of harmony, stop transforming as one united whole and become two mutually exclusive opposites instead. One starts doing the cha-cha and the other the can-can! This causes a riot and disfigures our creations.

One prominent example of this crazy dance happening in our society at the moment is where nature is perceived as separate to mankind, and we have lakes of floating plastic in our seas because of it.

This imbalance and distortion has also happened between the feminine and the masculine principle and directly impacts our expression of beauty.

Patriarchy: The Deep-Rooted Dance of Distortion

Our culture has had a long tradition of linking the feminine principle with what it means to be female and the masculine principle with what it means to be male. Patriarchy is the distorted system that has evolved from dominating and placing value over masculine attributes – such as power, control, rationality, competitiveness – and associating them with men. The nurturing, emotionally expressive, compassionate and receptive attributes of the feminine became inferior in this system – as did women.

The result of this disturbing dance is that it is constricting the way we express our beauty. As little girls, we've had our feet bound, our genitals mutilated; our breasts trained. As grown women we continue the self-harm; tucking our tummies, breaking our ribs, and torturing our bodies – the ugliest things have happened in the name of beauty.

These restrictive gender roles and the dominance of patriarchy have not only disfigured women physically, but have also impacted on their long-suffering relationship with beauty. It's become wounding work trying to epitomise the latest beauty ideal. I'm exhausted. How about you?

We can begin to reconcile this destructive dance by reclaiming beauty for ourselves and listening to her story and guidance. Let's evoke the four goddesses – Responsibility, Liberation, Courage, and Appreciation to help us do this. Together they act as the four pillars that uphold the integrity and inspiration of beauty.

The first of these is the Goddess of Responsibility.

The Goddess of Responsibility

Sing in me, Muse, sing in me, dance your creative breath into these words, and through me tell the story of that woman skilled in all ways of Responsibility...

The Goddess of Responsibility carries a Labrys – a double-headed 'moon axe' – as her instrument of knowledge. This is the emblem of the High Priestess, ruler of the divine feminine authority and governor of matriarchal power. Her role is to keep beauty balanced. She does this by questioning the status quo.

A treacherous plot has taken place in the kingdom of Responsibility. The Goddess has become hideously disfigured, her mouth is bleeding, and 'our' precious beauty is being held captive by the King of Patriarchy and his capitalist court, Consumption.

They now clasp the Labrys, keeping it cleverly disguised. We need to become the wild 'wonderwomen' who reclaim this weapon. We must become our own protectors; we have been gifted the responsibility for shaping our beauty, but it lies in the hands of Patriarchy.

How To 'Reconcile the Dance' and Reinstate Balance in Ourselves, Our Lives and Our Communities

As we know, the muse was traditionally female. It was the muse's job to penetrate the male artist with her inspiration, and bring forth an original work of art from his creative womb. She is the feminine creative energy that impregnates action. He then gives birth to his painting and she stretches, reclines, and lights a cigarette!

Can you see how the roles are blended and reversed here? She impregnates him. This exclusive relationship of the female impregnating the male brings equality and harmony between the masculine and feminine energies. Both are creators and both are responsible for the creation.

When we step into the role of artist and we have the primordial power of beauty as our muse, Beauty impregnates us, inspired into action we merge with her, and produce beauty from our creative womb. Et voila! The art we end up creating reflects our authentic expression of beauty and we can spot our truth. We also fall passionately in love with her and start to care deeply about her presence – we take responsibility for her.

Who Is Responsible for Beauty?

In today's image-conscious society our demand for the 'body beautiful' is extreme; diversity is simply 'out of fashion'. We live in an unattainable world of photoshopped heroines. Naomi Wolf claims that women have an impossible definition of "flawless beauty" to uphold, and makes the poignant point that "what women look like is considered important because what we say is not." Does being beautiful help us to get heard? Is the pressure of beauty silencing us? It is certainly shaping us. We are warping and distorting under the immense pressure to 'be beauty'.

Pause for a moment and honestly answer this question:

Who is responsible for creating your image at the moment?

Image is powerful: it sells us a feeling and can deliver an identity. Today's society provides women with a clothes rail of man-made 'beauty' images just waiting to be tried on – each one designed to illicit an emotional response from us. We spend hours in front of the mirror squeezing into these images, trying to glimpse our divine reflection. Then find it totally disheartening when we don't 'match up' to the standards and see or feel our beauty reflected back.

We are so busy refashioning our flesh to fit the ideal image that we've forgotten we have something significant to say. It's our unique creative expression of beauty that brings our message to the world, creates our eternal worth, and illuminates the divine within us. And our access to that lies beyond silky-smooth skin.

What Can We Do about It?

As women, we can unite together for change to take place. Let's remove the redundant lens of patriarchy from our tired eyes one final time. It has shredded our once revered union with its cut-throat blade of competition and comparison, and left us feeling alienated, excluded, threatened and drenched in shame.

When I was a tall, plump ten-year-old, I went to a friend's birthday party. Like many girls of this age, I had a desperate ache to be liked and accepted. I was maturing early and had shifted into that horrid 'in-between' stage of neither being a young girl nor a young woman – I was the ugly duckling. All the other girls were still young girls, small, petite and pretty. I can remember us playing a game and one girl suggested that we all get on the scales and weigh ourselves. When it came to my turn I refused. Dripping in my puddle of shame I was pushed and taunted for my vulnerability and difference and rejected from the flock.

Let's recognise the ugly duckling in all of us and coax her into fresh waters; the welcoming waters of the divine feminine. In the words of Margaret Atwood: *"water does not resist. Water flows. When you plunge your hand into it, all you feel is a caress. Water is not a solid wall, it will not stop you. But water always goes where it wants to go and nothing in the end can stand against it."* She goes on to say, *"if you can't go through an obstacle, go around it. Water does."* We have all felt persecuted and despised for our ugliness at some point in our lives. Embodying our flowing feminine energy will bring us home to our magnificent flock, to receive each other with outstretched wings and nestle down in a bed of togetherness, to remember and believe in our beauty of unity and embrace our feminine power once again. We can hold the space for each other to nurse our wounds, nurture our uniqueness and celebrate our differences.

True beauty does not and cannot be divided. Not only do we need to reclaim our 'entire' beauty, both the inner and outer; but we need to take back the word 'beauty' and iron out its creased meaning for ourselves. Let's say "no" to being the 'object of artificial beauty'. Let's take responsibility for all sides of beauty – receiving it, reflecting it and defining it. Only then we can reinstate Beauty to her rightful place as our unique and natural expression of the sacred within us all.

It's time to evoke the Goddess of Liberation to help us reclaim beauty for ourselves.

The Goddess of Liberation

Sing in me, Muse, sing in me, dance your creative breath into these words, and through me tell the story of that woman skilled in all ways of Liberty…

The Goddess of Liberty wears a golden laurel wreath on her head as her instrument of knowledge. This is the emblem of victory, glory and success. A gardener at heart, her role is to protect and tend to beauty's growth. She does by this by taking action.

Reclaiming Beauty

All is not as it seems in the kingdom of Liberation. The Goddess lies asleep in her crystal bed, spellbound with apathy. The court Jester with his shocking yellow hair and foul mouth is running amok. He has grabbed the golden laurel wreath and is dancing like a fool in front of the villagers. Shocked at his dishonour and blatant disregard, there is unrest rising throughout the land.

To set our beauty free we first have to reclaim it and redefine it for ourselves. When we do, it frees up our self-imposed and culturally dictated limits so that we can see and appreciate what we have to offer.

Spotting our beauty is all about what we choose to see and from which lens we look.

How To 'Look' for Your Beauty

Which is most important to you – being desired or expressing your desires?

The Masculine Gaze – Being Desired

Laura Mulvey first established the term "the male gaze" as a feminist film critic highlighting how the lens in Hollywood movies presents women as objects of male desire. Women are a "spectacle" to be looked at and give visual pleasure. And men do the looking.

John Berger in his book *Ways of Seeing* also says something similar – "men act, women appear". We watch ourselves being looked at as men watch. How we "appear" to others affects our success, which is why we are constantly judging ourselves.

This masculine gaze has become deeply embedded in our culture and is accepted by both men and women as standard or 'normal'. We look through this lens frequently. Even more so today, with the impact of social media, as we drape and position our bodies in front of the selfie camera to create the thinnest, most flawless and pleasing images of ourselves. In doing this, we restrict ourselves to one image.

How we are seen becomes our focus – not how we feel or act. And we know as Life Artists that wherever we place our focus, that's where our energy flows. This gaze leaves us waiting for the nod of approval and rewards us for how we appear. We're asked to only be the objects for other people's desire.

This gaze also creates an energy of shame and guilt for us when we do desire something – such as sex. Instead of asking outright for our needs to be met we have learnt manipulative, apologetic, or secretive behaviours to appear acceptable. This leaves no room for our own needs, desires and pleasures.

These days as women we have money, good jobs and businesses, and financial independence. Yet we still invest a huge amount of our time focused on how we are "appearing". You would think this gaze would have dissolved by now. But it's rapidly growing and our daughters, nieces and granddaughters are adopting it.

If we want to take action and create beautiful lives we need to be aware of the "male gaze", hidden in the depths of our culture and find an alternative – "the feminine gaze".

The Feminine Gaze – Expressing Your Desires

The feminine gaze is impregnated by the creative possibilities of life – this gaze has the answers we seek. We can become the subject of our gaze rather than the 'spectacle' to be looked at.

The feminine gaze is not so much about power or pleasure – it is about your presence. If you focus on your own pleasure, your needs and your desires, you can fulfil them and expand your presence – the sound of your existence in the universe, your shining sun. Bringing forth your unique presence in the world will help you to take up your space and see your potential. You become the storyteller, saying, *"I belong. Feel into me. I matter."*

We can see that the male gaze reduces you to a single image, whereas the female gaze liberates you and asks that you show up and be counted. With beauty as your muse you can look with the gaze of the feminine to receive beauty, then draw upon your will and action to bring your creations into being. This is how you can reclaim beauty. We are too used to being looked at. Now we must do the looking, we must take action and see it.

Woman have been seen as 'objets d'art' for a very long time – from femme fatale to Holy Virgin. The tightly-corseted roles, offered up for us to wear, restrict and squash our presence. It's time to adopt the role of the artist and construct healthy and meaningful images for ourselves.

Reclaiming beauty through the feminine has the ability to bring a time of peace, ecological balance, and harmony between the sexes, as well as nations. We can create a future that helps all women, children, and men flourish.

If we all create our original beauty we can contribute to the growth of the cosmos – reflect back its awe-inspiring beauty. The vitality of the whole will be seen and can drive new life.

With the feminine gaze as your guide you are liberated and can move forward to redefine the image of beauty for yourself – you can craft your original Creative Curves, which I call the "C" Curves. This will bring harmony and pleasure into your life.

Redefining Beauty

The S Curve

At the moment, our image is being outlined by the sneaky 'S' Curve – a concept taken from traditional Greek sculpture. It is when the body is positioned in a sinuous, off-balance stance, and takes the form of an S shape.

This S Curve was adopted and developed by the fashion industry and used to define the shape of all beautiful women. Women's curves were tightly bound in corsets, which pushed the abdomen back, threw the breasts forward and arched the back. This was a way of emphasising the 'natural' difference between men and women – large breasts, tiny waists and large hips. It also promoted the notion of women being defined in relation to men. Women were restricted in movement, shoved off balance, and forced to take tiny shallow breaths. In their helpless restriction, they were tamed and desirable.

Today our curves are tolerated if we have small hips, a tiny waist, but large breasts. To achieve this, we have the freedom to wear Wonderbras and Spanx pants and we pretty much have the autonomy to wear anything we want. Or so, it would seem.

Yet, the ideal S Curve silhouette still prevails in form and still carries the restrictive imbalance in its energetic imprint. We know it well; it's a common pose used in fashion photography with the body in an S position with one shoulder tilted towards the extended hip. The body weight is positioned on the leg under the extended hip.

We enact variations of this S shape in many of our habitual postures today.

And in doing so, we take up less space, we keep our legs together and our elbows in to appear physically smaller. We imbalance ourselves by putting our weight onto one leg, thrusting out our hips and arching our backs, or crossing our legs and sitting with our weight on one hip.

By the time I was twelve, I'd learnt to cross my legs when sitting, because it made my thighs look thinner. I also learnt that by sticking my hips and chest out I would receive male attention and feel significant.

It wasn't until I started to work with my body – actor training, dance classes, singing lessons, and then again with yoga, that I understood just how imbalanced, restricted, and 'shrunk' I'd become. I still find it feels 'unnatural' to sit with both feet on the ground and instantly want to cross a leg or put a foot up. The terrifying feeling of having two large squashed thighs in front of me is still embedded. Although now I think about how my strong legs have carried me around the world, walked away from excruciating pain, trekked mountains to see gorillas, and danced me into a pleasurable trance. I love every squishy bit of them!

The S curve may not be shrinking our waistline anymore, but it is shrinking our energetic presence. And it's something we need to be aware of if we want to feel the full sense of our power and expand our vibration. You will have a chance to investigate and experiment with your presence and postures in Part Two.

The 'C' Curve

Your conscious creative choice that shapes culture.

Women are active participants in the cultural forces that shape masculine and feminine ideals. In fact, we reinforce it when we maintain the status quo and view ourselves and others from the restrictive masculine gaze.

There is another way. You can reshape your sexuality and feminine identity with the 'C' Curve, your conscious creative choice. Your 'C' Curves are unique to you. Irresistible, sensual, sexual, soft, gentle and inviting, they are an invitation for you to embody your source of power. Your 'C' Curves can protect your growth as well as feed and nourish your life – no matter what size they are. They bring you balance, freedom and expansion. Honour them, wear them with pride, spread your legs and take up your celestial space.

When you unleash your unknown, untamed 'C' curves you are on fire. Burning to express, you embellish creative femininity. Your sexuality is no longer shaped by the passive, outdated mould. As you discover your pleasures, you effortlessly become multi-orgasmic – scenting your creative nectar on all you touch. But this is a side effect.

All that energy you once wasted on being desirable is now channelled into your creative desires. Your sexual instinct is owned by you and is a poetic expression of your divinity. You can 'feel into' yourself. This rich experience of touching your primal beauty takes you beyond orgasm, beyond your body and lifts the veil into other worlds.

Let's unleash our 'C' Curves, get creative with our femininity, say no to repression and no to exploitation, and carve the path for other women to do the same.

To make this happen we will need to summon the Goddess of Courage.

The Goddess of Courage

Sing in me, Muse, sing in me, dance your creative breath into these words, and through me tell the story of that woman skilled in all ways of Courage...

The Goddess of Courage holds the staff of Asclepius in her left hand. This serpent-entwined rod is her instrument of knowledge. This is the emblem of medicine, renewal and wisdom. A wise warrior at heart, it is her role to protect and tend to beauty's health, which she does by caring deeply about authenticity.

The Goddess of Courage got wind of the appalling news of the mimicking court jester and the spellbound Liberty; she is compelled to protect beauty's originality. Courage has departed on horseback and her kingdom sits empty, cold and dark. She now stands weeping aside Liberty's bed, frantically trying to wake her with her trusty staff.

Dare To Be Different

The Goddess of Courage can wake up and shake up your beauty. She is your pillar of support to embrace your healthy authentic power. Your exclusive gifts are illuminated and shared when you evoke her. You can glimpse your tremendous power. Whatever seems impossible is made possible when you risk her magic. She is the motivator you need for creating your art and filling it with your beauty.

Original Beauty Versus Manufactured Beauty

I recently visited the Uffizi Gallery in Florence, excited to see Botticelli's painting *The Birth of Venus*. Picture the scene – bustling crowds of tourists, endless queues and lots of dripping sweat – hardly beautiful!

Venus had metamorphosed into clichéd keyrings, fridge magnets, mugs and posters before I even stepped inside the building. "Do I really need to see the original work of art now?" I questioned, as the smell of pizza wafted past.

With my romantic notion slightly tainted, I eventually walked into the room housing the painting. As soon as I stood in front of it, I felt an expanding of my awareness, butterflies in my stomach, and I was unexpectedly moved to tears.

This physical reaction was a response from my soul as it felt the original energy held in this sublime masterpiece. The painting represents the birth of love and spiritual beauty as the driving force of life; I experienced this beauty intensely and was moved by it. All these centuries after it was created, the energy retained within the painting's form is still speaking to souls that listen.

The power of truth that original beauty transfers, compared to artificial or manufactured beauty, is quite incredible; it's even more astounding the way we are wired up to recognise it.

But we must take the risk and put it out there. We must dare to share our art.

Dare To Share

To make yourself beautiful to your eyes you will need to rise up, reveal yourself and dare to dream. Unearth the courage and discipline to parade your 'C' Curves, show up fully and do every act to the best of your ability at the time. When you do something with a heart full of passion, you and others will find beauty in it.

When Scottish singer Susan Boyle turned up on the *Britain's Got Talent* stage in 2009, the audience and judges were cynical and judgmental of her image. She didn't look the part of a 'typical' star performer.

She then opened her mouth and sang *I Dreamed a Dream* from *Les Misérables* and blew everyone away with her sublime voice. Her beauty was recognised internationally as it touched souls and opened hearts everywhere. She was accepted and revered. She became her own work of art because she dared to show up, be her authentic self, and show us her gifts, no matter what others thought or said about her.

Five Ways To Help You Dare

1. Embrace Yourself as Creator
When you take the position of artist you become the creator of your beauty, you define it, empower it and are liberated by it. By embracing the artist within, you can recover your innate beauty and explore your relationship with it.

2. See Your Beauty in Its Entirety
Our obsession with our outer beauty is a massive distraction away from our soul's desire and our empowerment. Our value, meaning and purpose are much more than this.

Stay focused on the beauty of your body, your mind, and your soul as one interconnected whole. Feel your way in. Beauty is experienced as a feeling; give yourself time to get used to this feeling, where and how is it felt and expressed for you. What is its relationship to your pleasure?

3. Own Your Vision
By exploring your relationship to beauty, you become the object of your personal pleasure; you can validate yourself by your own criteria. The essence of your beauty does not depend on the ticking time bomb of youth. Instead, it grows and alters with you.

You are always free to sketch out your own vision of personal beauty and step into it. This "damned if we are, damned if we're not" outlook on beauty is a burden we can release. When we do we will reflect our true beauty.

4. Remember Your Connections
As little girls we were sold the story that we need to consume

to create our desire, consume to have worth, consume to feel secure; this ranges from consuming the prince with vast wealth for eternal love to consuming our beauty from a bottle.

This greedy consumption cycle has left the majority of us women feeling empty and bland – hating our bodies, and feeling stupid and useless after a certain age. If our connections to nature and energy are strong, we will remember to tune into our soul to create our beauty. Remember that you are wired to create beauty – your extraordinary beauty.

5. Unite with Your Tribe

Patriarchal Beauty has perpetuated competitiveness amongst women, keeping them separate and isolated from each other. The 'fat talk', the 'not good enough' speech, and the comparisons, don't serve any of us.

Instead, let us unite with our tribe, provide an inspiring space for beauty to be all inclusive, create together, paint each other's faces, appreciate each other as an ever-growing work of art.

Let's summon the Goddess of Appreciation to help us unite, see the beauty in all things, and illuminate our soul's joy.

The Goddess of Appreciation

Sing in me, Muse, sing in me, dance your creative breath into these words, and through me tell the story of that woman skilled in all ways of Appreciation...

The Goddess of Appreciation holds the torch of fire as her instrument of knowledge. This is the emblem of illumination and clarity. A visionary and leader, her role is to protect and tend to Beauty's pleasure. She does this by looking.

Just when the Goddess Courage felt she could do no more to wake the sleeping Liberty, she heard the soulful song of

Appreciation rise up. The Goddess Appreciation stood in awe of the Goddess Courage, and her enchanting gaze activated Courage's trusty staff.

At this moment, the Goddess Liberty awoke and rose high from her bed, like the Phoenix from the ashes. From her elevated position, she could see the blood dripping from the face of Responsibility. Her heart sank. She went to the Goddess and kissed her gently on the mouth. The tender kiss healed and empowered the Goddess Responsibility, and she felt secure to overthrow King Patriarchy and release Beauty from the clutches of Consumption.

The Goddess of Appreciation can show you how to widen your perception and see beauty in everything; she breeds inclusivity and togetherness. She is an angel-headed hipster, shaking her tail-feather and helping you to find your groove. Listen out for her song – it is the call of beauty.

Why Should We Appreciate Beauty?

Beauty is like a social media network for souls; providing the space for them to share, connect up, and appreciate each other. If we spent as much time appreciating beauty as we do on Facebook – our lives would feel incredibly special!

If you take the time to get to know beauty's nature and appreciate her, your soul will be nourished and you will feel beautiful.

Do you remember at the beginning of the book we explored the importance of your Soul's Joy? It shines the light and acts as a guide for your life's direction, alerting you to your gifts, your lessons, and your essence. Well, beauty speaks directly to your soul and acts as a continuous invitation for you to hear the call of your soul's joy.

This is the genius of beauty. She is a bringer of truths – a reflection of the sacred; both universally and individually. It is in this way that she unites and connects humanity.

What Can We Learn from Beauty?

Do you remember the Sun Goddess Amaterasu who was enticed out of her cave by laughter, merriment and others taking pleasure? Well, when we are in our caves, clinging like vines to everything around us, strangling our life force and hiding our sun, beauty is the muse that can entice us out of our darkness. She is our merriment – our pleasure.

Once we are out, our world lights up and we can see our reflection. Beauty asks you to take delight in her and she illuminates your truth. What you find beautiful is a reflection of your personality and your individuality – you can discover your true nature in what you find beautiful.

How Does Beauty Entice You Out of the Cave?

Beauty's nature is transcendent. She knocks you out with the blissful sublime – where something is so overwhelming that it consumes or obliterates your sense of self. You feel your part in the Great Mosaic. Every time we feel a little wobbly and become underwhelmed with life, we can look for beauty to remind us of our place in the bigger picture.

This is why creating your art is not only a benefit to you, but also for others. By sharing your art and having them appreciate it, you remind them of their greatness – you provide them with soul food.

Soul Food

Beauty is powerful. She can communicate over distance, imparting something of herself to those who see her. Beauty is visible to both the physical eye and the eye of the soul. This double visibility is a unique link between the worlds. She is a bridge for our soul's expression and offers transformation from sense to form.

Every time we create from our soul, we incarnate a part of our true essence. Our original beauty is held in a form and expressed for others to see. This power is why many of us are intimidated by and feel vulnerable about our creative expression.

I sang in a blues and soul band for many years with my sister, Kate. Now, over the 19 years we performed together we sang many different songs. Some were amazing and some just OK. But there was this one song she used to sing that made the hairs on the back of your neck prickle, your skin tingle; the way she sang it made something inside you rise with emotion every single time. It was like a conversation among souls was taking place between her and the audience.

Her vocals would courageously 'blast it out' from the depths of her soul, and each time it simultaneously embodied part of her unique essence. Yet it transcends beyond her and stands alone as a 'beautiful song'. This experience was understood and shared with all who listened. This effect is original beauty in action, and this is what makes exceptional music, art, theatre, and this is also the same ingredient required for a nourished soul and an enchanting life.

Finding Your Set of Aesthetics

The Nature and Appreciation of Beauty

You are the visionary of your life. As you spend time with Beauty and explore her as your Muse you will devise your own personal set of aesthetics. Until then, here's a few to get you started.

The visionary looks from fresh angles and finds endless vantage points to merge with Beauty.

Try these 5 ways to help you appreciate beauty.

1. Remove the Glasses, Whip Off the Lenses, and Merge

Beauty has a habit of striking us with her sublime feeling and then we have a habit of judging and reasoning away her experience. By removing judgment and comparison from beauty, we are left with her essence. Feel and accept the sense of awe that she brings, rather than judge, because the feeling of awe will enchant your life.

2. *Notice the Beauty of Others*

Even if we don't share the same aesthetic taste as another, we can recognise the beauty offered up in their art and have respect for its expression. If we pay attention to their creations we can witness their truth which will, on a deeper level, reflect ours.

3. *Turn on Your Night Vision*

There is beauty in the dark night of the soul; by seeing death you value life. By seeking beauty in our dark times, we learn lessons and discover hidden gifts. Meaning, purpose and value is increased. The Life Artist can build beautiful things out of her sufferings, as well as her joy.

When you look for beauty you are not looking to coat over dark situations, you are looking to see genius in each situation. Finding the beauty in all things – even our disowned darkest experiences – can be challenging, but it will help us to grow and see our life lessons.

Beauty exists in all things – even elephant dung has intricate patterns in it.

4. *'Awe for One and One for Awe'*

Become an 'Awe' Musketeer! We all need more 'wow' moments. Awe is the number one emotion for the Life Artist and there is a good reason for this. 'Awesome' experiences have inspired countless works of art – they stimulate and intensify our creativity.

The feeling of awe stops us in our tracks and is time-expanding. It helps to diminish our sense of self and guides us to see outside of ourselves. Our thinking gains flexibility, and we can drop our limiting beliefs. This shows us new insights;

we are able to connect different perspectives and see beyond our present situation. And this, of course, is how our creativity is inspired. Experiences of awe can be transformative and life-changing.

Awe leads to a perception that the world is good, beautiful and desirable. Awe leads you to beauty and beauty leads you to awe, which is a great cycle for you to be in. It offers you hope and injects magic into life. Having regular awe experiences also keeps your circle of life balanced and reminds you that spirit is at your centre.

Awe is the wizard that helps us engage with life from a place of joy, wonder, and gratitude. Creating beauty will help you to see your own awesomeness.

If you're feeling stuck and need an 'awe fix' head to Nature – she is the master of awesome experiences.

5. Nurture Beauty

Become the great Mother of beauty. Allow your creative womb to generate and shield beauty, your breasts to feed her, and your arms to embrace and comfort her. In return you will receive the gifts of nourishment, protection, and transformation. Enter into a continual cycle of death and rebirth with her. When you become the Mother, you will be shown your creative life-breeding patterns.

Active nurturing can show you how to appreciate and care for your beauty, to slow down, take time to tend to yourself and receive your creations, to recognise your inner longing and follow it, wherever it leads you. This will stop you getting stuck in one image.

Nurturing beauty will bring you pleasure and delight. And provide a deep sense of belonging; you find yourself in the place you have longed to be.

Take Your Praise

Find your extraordinary beauty and astonish yourself.

Beauty is the Life Artist's asset that grows with time – bring on the awestruck wrinkles!

Beauty as your Muse links your spiritual and aesthetic experiences. She exalts your sun so that you can shine and offers you a way to grow and transcend. In the process, she fulfils your soul's longing and provides access to the mystery of life, which fills your world with meaning.

Through beauty's presence you have an open invitation to live an enchanted life. Just like nature, we are called to create beauty and to cultivate her. We are invited to let beauty penetrate our heart, and to respond to her by creating further beauty in our own lives.

Creating beauty is how we expand the mosaic pattern to reflect its truth. Beauty the inspirer has the ability to break through your ugly and restrictive patterns. She activates the portal of your imagination; so that you may enter mystic worlds.

Can you survive the vision of your own beauty reflected back?

I urge you to take the risk to see your wonder. Don't be the Supernova – the star that implodes violently into itself. You have the choice to implode violently or shine your beauty brightly and leave your legacy on the planet for your children, grandchildren, and their grandchildren.

Leave them the enchantment of life.

Visions of Beauty

Try sketching out a few different images of your own vision of beauty to step into.

1. Create a sacred space where you won't be disturbed and gather some colouring pencils and paper together.
2. Set your intent to discover the question, "What is MY vision of beauty?"
3. Take a few moments to tune into your feelings; 'feel into yourself' and still your heart from emotion. When you feel ready start to play and sketch your vision.
4. Play: If you don't know where to start, choose your favourite colour and start to draw some shapes. If you are confident at drawing – get stuck in. Don't worry about 'getting it wrong', you'll learn just as much through what you don't like as what you do.
5. Explore your feelings: After you have produced a few different images. Explore what you like or dislike about them. Consider colour, shape, balance, texture, symmetry. Also reflect on how you felt in the process. Did the perfectionist in you rise up? Remember your beauty is not about perfection, she is about your presence.
6. Create a new image: Choose all the bits you like from the previous sketches and create another image. Consider if what you found beautiful before was because of its relation to other shapes, colours or the space surrounding it.

Look at your end image and reflect once more using the following questions:

- Have I changed the image to be more pleasing for others' idea of beauty or for myself?
- Who/what is defining my outline?
- Who/what created my ideal beauty?
- Who/what is deciding what my experience of beauty is?
- Does this image give me pleasure?
- Does it arouse and sustain my interest?

As you have explored, feasting on Nature, energy and beauty will plump up your roots of existence, sculpting them to nourish the exquisite art of you.

Nature feeds your belonging, energy feeds your quality of life and beauty feeds your soul. Together they are your cosmic power.

Now that you have filled your roots with the fine dining of life, you are ready to unfold the art of you. Let's delve into Part Two – The Living Bridges.

Snippets of Wisdom

Beauty is my birthright,
it reflects the truth of who I am.

Part II

The Living Bridges: Shaping Your Roots

The Pilgrimage to the Living Root Bridges

The Artist is no other than he who unlearns what he has learned, in order to know himself.
EE Cummings

As I took my first of 3,000 steps into the depths of the Khasi jungle, my soul fluttered alongside the butterflies... I knew this journey would grow in my heart forever. I was entering a place where myths and legends swelled from the land and time ticked only in the mind. I had crossed into other worlds. Here the waterfalls created soothing pools of tickling turquoise and bridges grew from the earth.

I couldn't quite believe I had made it here. This place had been on my radar for a while, and I didn't know why. I'd seen a programme about a place known as 'the wettest place on earth.' I know, it doesn't sound very inviting! And when I read how to get to this 'abode in the clouds' it all seemed far too complicated. Yet, the nagging feeling didn't go away. So, a couple of years later here I was, standing in a rainforest in north-east India, searching for the unknown.

I had come to see the Living Root Bridges. These are the finest example of Nature and humans working harmoniously together and they are exquisite works of art in their own right. Don't get me wrong, these are purely practical structures. Because heavy rainfall regularly washed away all their bamboo bridges, the Khasi tribes discovered an ingenious way to make their bridges strong and permanent; they started sculpting them from the roots of trees. This requires immense patience. They must regularly nurture and tend to the roots. It can take 15 to 20 years for the root bridge structure to reach the other side of the bank – about the same time it takes us to grow into adults. Because they are alive and growing, the bridges continue to gain strength over time. Some of them are around 500 years old.

My journey to the Living Bridges became a pilgrimage; every step along the way offered challenge and insight that led me to merge with Nature and understand my significance and spiritual connection further. One of the biggest lessons I learnt was to 'get out of my own way' so that my soul could receive the pleasure of the moment and my spirit could soar. In the rainforest, your potential truly unfolds with every step. It has to for your survival.

The Art of the Living Bridges

We all have our own living bridges. As we grow our life experiences shape our roots of existence – we are cultivated and guided to grow in specific directions along the way. If we look at our lives, with an artful eye on each of our roots, we can see clearly what is original, what requires attention and what can be reshaped to reveal our true selves.

As a Life Artist, most of your suffering will arise from your internal struggle to discover, appreciate and express yourself – to hold up your sun and shine it. Getting to know who you truly are is a lifelong journey, and with every step, the opportunity to love yourself is presented. Grab this opportunity with the whole of your heart.

This part of the book offers you four Living Bridges to explore. As you step onto each bridge, you will discover worlds rich in possibility and support. The entire journey is a process of illuminating your shadows in order to contour your light. This is how you 'get out of your own way' to see your true nature and learn the skills to create your life consciously.

Try approaching this part as if it is a personal pilgrimage – a journey to unravel your sacred beauty and unleash your unknown potential. Use your Living Bridges to create a balance between your mind, body and soul and to keep your presence aligned. The more you use them, the deeper and stronger they – and you – will become.

Chapter 6

The Living Bridge of Theatre

Let's paint a picture....

How the Philistines Discovered Theatre

You've bought your programme entitled *How the Philistines Discovered Theatre* and some tasty ice cream. The usher shows you to your seat in the stalls, a disappointing position, but the tickets were much cheaper. After apologetically clambering over many bodies and luckily avoiding the tall man with the hat, you turn off your mobile phone and wait with rising anticipation.

The curtain rises to reveal the stage and the backdrop of hot desert sands. A few cacti are scattered around, some mysterious old bones are laid in a circle to the left, and to the right is some burnt grass.

There is a stomping sound, some gruff grunts and much heavy breathing. Two rather hairy-looking characters enter stage left. Their hunched bodies are smeared with mud and their modesty covered with animal skins. The first of the two – the sweaty one with the bone necklace – stretches his hands in the air and yawns. He goes straight to the front of the stage, sits down on a pile of sand, wipes the sweat from his brow, closes his eyes and lightly snores.

The second character drags his feet distractedly as he slowly makes his way over to the pile of burnt grass. At first he looks puzzled. Cautiously he fondles and sniffs the burnt grass; it instantly falls to bits in his large hands.

Scratching his head and his bottom, he turns his body to look at his snoring brother. In a deep-toned voice, he grunts, "Flog, wake up." Flog snores more loudly.

In a louder and now high-pitched, whiney tone he says: "Flog, our wheat is burnt again. It's too hot, Floggy. What are we going to do? The children haven't eaten for a week."

Flog shuffles a little in the sand and releases a frustrated snore.

Trog gathers the rest of the burnt wheat in his arms and walks towards Flog.

He whispers loudly in his ear: "The elder women are getting angry. You remember what happened to you last time we arrived back empty-handed from gathering the harvest?"

Flog immediately jumps up from his sleep, covered in sand and now sweating profusely. He repeatedly paces the stage from left to right. He notices the circle of old bones and stands in the middle of them. Trog sits down outside the circle and watches Flog.

Flog scratches his head. He starts pacing anxiously in a repeated pattern of steps. The music kicks in and it's the backing track to Edwin Starr's *War*. Flog throws his hands up in the air and in a hopeful tone says: "God, rain, when is it coming? Now?" "God, rain, when is it coming? Now?" "God, rain, when is it coming? Now?" "God, rain, when is it coming? Now?"

He smiles to himself as his steps become lighter and firmer, his body taller, his speech louder as he starts to chant: "God, rain, when is it coming? Now?" "God, rain, when is it coming? Now?" "God, rain, when is it coming? Now?"

Trog nods his head, enjoying the sounds and the movements Flog is making.

Flog starts spinning faster and faster. "God, rain, when is it coming? Now? God, rain, when is it coming? Now? God, rain, when is it coming? Now? God, rain, when is it coming? Now?"

He suddenly stands very still, stares directly at you and says: "There's absolutely nothing…"

Trog suddenly jumps up, giggles and holds out his hand as if feeling something, he looks upwards and says: "Say it again!"

He moves quickly to join Flog in the circle and imitates his pattern of movement and speech.

"God, rain, when is it coming? Now!"

The sound of rain increases and they dance ecstatically. Flog falls to his knees sobbing and says: "Oh dear rain spirit, thank you for answering."

Trog hugs his brother and says: "The women will be so happy with you, I mean us, Flog. We have discovered such a power. It's magic – a way to talk to the gods so they listen and reply. We can teach this to our sons and they too can please the women folk."

The curtain falls and you quickly make a dash for the toilet before the queues start.

What Does the Living Bridge of Theatre Offer the Life Artist?

All the World's a Stage and all the men and women merely players.
William Shakespeare

The roots of theatre developed from the enactment of ritual and ceremony, which is one way of directing, experiencing and communicating with spirit. Our tribal ancestors discovered theatre's ability to bridge worlds many years ago. With its powerful influence, they could worship nature, speak to the gods, shapeshift into other beings, share valuable information easily among the community, and ultimately, bring more nourishment and beauty to life.

Theatre not only reflects a way of communing with the gods but it also mirrors our lives – the way we take action, express ourselves and communicate our truth. The theatre holds worlds of possibility. We can view ourselves as the actor, the director, the stage manager, set designer – the opportunities are endless. And just like ourselves, the stage has a front and back area – an internal and external world. When we become aware of these countless reflections we realise our deeper truths and the meaning of our existence. We come to understand the point of it all! You can use this sacred knowledge to create a fulfilling and soul-centred life.

How Can You Use It To Unfold the Art of You?

Stepping onto the Living Bridge of Theatre will widen your point of view and help you to bring awareness to your actions, which is the first step to bringing your vision to life.

Theatre in its original art form embodies the entirety of human experience: the patterns that create our realities, the stories we tell, the masks we wear and the environments we live in. It is a vital resource of us to reclaim. It is your unique expression of your presence that makes you come alive on Earth's sacred stage. With Nature as your backdrop, you are given three instruments to play out your part and express your story – your mind, your body and your soul.

Theatre holds a mirror up to your sacred stage. If you don't like what you see in the mirror, you have the ability to transform the image into one of truth. You can create a beautiful vision of yourself and your life.

We already explored in Part One how every action we take makes a difference to our lives and the lives of others by adding to and influencing the star-studded mosaic of consciousness. The world of theatre can provide you with insight and detail into how you are using your actions to shape your life. Nothing can happen on the stage without action; even silence is a conscious action on the stage. By placing yourself metaphorically and physically on a stage, you can bring awareness to all of your actions and non-actions. In doing so, you open to a world of many possibilities; you can clearly see which actions to take to cultivate your presence and create meaning, beauty and purpose in your life.

Let's get started...

The Theatre of Mind

Point of View

Your point of view is the way you are seeing the world and it projects your reality. It is entangled deep within your ancestral roots of curling core values and bulging beliefs that are stitched in place by your parents, their parents, cultures, authorities and experiences. Unravelling these ancient roots will help to expand your perception.

In the theatre, the point of view an actor takes drives her character's actions. As actors, we examine the point of view of the whole character to understand their truth. We question the authentic expression of the mind, body and soul by looking to see if they are speaking the same truth. This congruent harmony is essential to express your natural and beautiful self.

To retrain and shift the roots of your point of view, you need to be aware of them and know what they are. Sometimes they can be so deeply embedded that it takes a strong experience to shift them at root level.

Do you own your point of view and trust it? How is your point of view driving your actions?

Let's delve into a little bit of Shakespeare to find out. There is great truth embedded in his art, which many of us are playing out in our lives today.

Is Your Life Really 'As You Like It'?

Have you been reduced to an unsmiling set of bones?

Are you jumping through hoops to satisfy some rite of passage, created by a world over which you seem to have no influence?

Are you tired of being the tragic heroine believing there is a terrible flaw in your nature that stops you succeeding? Are you enslaved by a war in your mind that won't let you sleep? Are you fed up with being doomed by your internal conflict?

You've been playing the Dane!

If you haven't come across this expression, it's given to those actors who play Shakespeare's Danish character, Hamlet. In the thespian world, this honour marks a prestigious benchmark in an actor's career. Hamlet was a troubled, complex character, challenging to portray and definitely something to get your acting teeth into.

It seems these days we don't need to be an exceptionally skilled actor to 'play the Dane'. There are many of us wandering around with heads in our hands playing the role to perfection.

You see, Hamlet's conflict between his inner and outer worlds causes his rejection of life. His tragic flaw is his inability to trust his point of view and take action. His anxiety develops from working so hard to gather all the information he needs to make the right choices in life, to do the 'right' thing and to be seen acting in the 'right' way.

The tragedy of his own self-doubt, indecisiveness and internal conflict paralyses him, and he 'cannot' change his situation. He knows that he should act on what he knows, but he keeps struggling to understand more, hoping to discover certainty – the ultimate truth – before he has to act.

He is a tormented mind. But part of him knows that he's doing the wrong thing by not taking action. And so, guilt-ridden he sabotages his life further by constantly criticising and belittling himself, yet still never changing his situation or doing anything about it.

At the end of the play, we see the famous image of Hamlet holding up the court jester Yorick's skull. He symbolically holds up his access to happiness, merriment and laughter while he realises all the stuff he's worried about is a total illusion; wealth and status have no meaning after death. The pleasure of life is transient – it can be found only in the moment.

Hamlet dies before getting a chance to express his truth and someone else has to do it for him. Unfortunately, we don't have this saving grace – only you can express your truth.

Have You Been Playing the Dane?

How many times have you found yourself in Hamlet's situation? Expending all your energy worrying, needing certainty and normality before taking pleasure in life's splendid moments, or making the changes necessary for you "to be or not to be"?

Not sure? Try rereading the following explanation of Hamlet and replace you name with his…

Vanessa... is a tormented mind. But part of her knows that she's doing the wrong thing by not taking action. And so, guilt-ridden, she sabotages her life further by constantly criticising and belittling herself, yet still never changing her situation or doing anything about it.

Actually, the above statement summed me up perfectly before I had my Alchemy Moment in 2003 and faced the death of a lifelong dream, the death of my marriage, the death of my identity and the (almost) death of my husband. Like Hamlet I was paralysed with fear and anxiety trying to do the right thing. My soul was urging me to change the situation, but I didn't. It took an extremely strong life experience for my point of view to shift so that I might be true to myself.

A Few Words on Conflict and Death

Theatre requires conflict and tension for the play to have meaning and progression, for it to be exciting and keep us on the edge of our seats. Life is also like this. If we remember conflict is there to be resolved – to learn from, to keep us hooked on life and growing wholeheartedly – it liberates us to take action, follow our heart's desire and deal with challenging situations head on.

When we are closest to death we often feel the most alive – think about a roller coaster ride or galloping on a stallion. Death asks us to look beyond what we know to something greater than ourselves. It shows us the impermanence of life; it teaches us to respect life and live each moment fully. Remembering our only certainty in life is death starts to make life very precious indeed. It brings conscious awareness and gratitude to the present moment, helps you to use your time wisely, and is one way to focus your mind and body to act on the direction of your soul.

High in the Himalayan mountains of Ladakh, in the town of Leh, I stumbled upon a graffiti wall – a bit like the town's bucket list that all the villagers can write on. It says: "Before I die..." and they finish the sentence with what they'd love to do. Some have written "have a child", others "to want less materialistic things" and some "to travel the world". This is a lovely way to share and stimulate our dreams and be aware of our own mortality on the planet.

Many of us have bucket lists and dreams we wish to follow, but like Hamlet we find excuses to not take action – our job, finances, partner, ill health or kids. We lack the courage to step into the unknown and take a risk; we want a guarantee that we are doing the right thing, and so, we resist taking action.

Do you remember David Hawkins' Scale of Consciousness model that we briefly looked at in Part One? He discovered that the level of courage was a critical turning point in leading you towards truth. Courage empowers you. You stop pulling from the negative energy field because you stop projecting and believing that the source of your power comes from outside of yourself. You start to appreciate your internal power and attract this; you feel able to cope with challenging situations that arise, your body feels strong and your consciousness expands.

To Be Or Not To Be?

How can you find the courage to take action?
The question for Hamlet that haunts him throughout his performance is the famous line "to be or not to be" – whether to continue to exist or not.

It's a really empowering question to ask ourselves. Am I existing in a life I no longer need, wish for, or desire? Do I want to spend a lifetime existing? Or can I let go and live fully now? Can I choose another life, another role, another stage – one where I can play the starring role perhaps?

What Would I Do If I Had Six Months To Live?
My whole life changed when I asked myself this simple question,

answered it, and followed up the answer with action. I urge you to try it.

Answering this question honestly can shift your perception and your life.

It helps you to identify what areas of your life you are happy with, or not.

- It brings gratitude for what you do have.
- It supports you in finding your heart's desire.
- It sets you on a path of empowerment and self-love.
- It shows you where you are placing your values.
- It brings self-respect and trust.
- It reveals your fears and beliefs.
- It reveals illusions that you are living.
- It shows you possibility and potential.

Try the following exercise:
Take yourself to a nourishing environment where you won't be disturbed. Your wild space you developed in Chapter 2 is perfect.

Set the intent: *I wish to hear guidance from my soul* and ask the following question:

What would I do if I had six months to live?

Write, doodle and note down any physical sensations, feelings, images, thoughts and answers.

What stops you from doing this?

Is your point of view limiting you? If so, try this quick exercise to explore your perspective:

Write down three statements that would stop you from doing this. Make sure each statement starts with I can't.

Here's an example of mine:

- I can't afford to go travelling
- I can't give up my job
- I can't travel alone

Now cross out the word 'can't' and replace it with won't':

- I 'won't' be able to afford to go travelling
- I 'won't' give up my job
- I 'won't' travel alone

How does this make you feel? Again write, doodle and note down any physical sensations, feelings and thoughts.

Rephrasing your statements from 'I can't' to 'I won't' transfers you from a victim position to the more empowering position of choice. This helps you to see your truth, take responsibility for your feelings, thoughts and desires and attract a positive energy field. It also supports you to find creative solutions to any limiting beliefs holding you back and encourages you to take healthy risks.

Finally, cross out the words 'I won't' and change them to 'I want':

- 'I want' to be able to afford to go travelling
- 'I want' to give up my job
- 'I want' to travel alone

How does this make you feel? Again write, doodle and note down any physical sensations, feelings and thoughts.

You may feel liberated and feel a flutter of excitement by acknowledging your desires. On the other hand, you may discover that you really don't want to give up your job, in which case you can appreciate your job or work around this – maybe go part-time, ask for a sabbatical or take unpaid leave. Either way, you become aware of your point of view and can start to direct your energy in the area you want to go and take action to achieve it.

The Theatre of Body

Presence

In Part One we explored the premise that your presence is the unique signal you transmit out to the cosmos and your power lies in expressing all you do with your full presence. Your full presence is revealed when you are fully present in your body and is expressed through your body in the way you breathe, move, speak, listen, think and feel.

From a layperson's point of view, presence can seem like an elusive quality to define. But all of us can recognise it; we notice when someone walks into the room exuding their full presence – they are literally beaming. Our heads turn and we are drawn to their magnetism, like a moth to a flame.

We are all born with presence, so why do some people seem to have much more of it than others?

We can find the answer by asking the infinite question again:

"To be or not to be?"

Shall I play my truth with full authenticity or not?

When you are shining your presence there is a lively quality to your energy – it's childlike and motivating – you feel light.

You have a choice to tap into this quality and be fully in your emotional, intellectual and spiritual presence. *To be* fully 'you'. Or you can choose *not to be*. You have a choice to stay present. In any given moment, your presence can be withdrawn, covered up, or projected fully. It's up to you and how you choose to be. The trouble is that most of us aren't aware of how we do this.

A good actor seeks to play the truth, they cultivate their presence to 'come alive' and be truthful on stage. As we discovered in Part One, this is also how our bodies are strengthened and we are empowered in our lives. We want to play our truth with full authenticity because it brings our sacred art to life.

Your presence can be cultivated very simply. Let's delve into the actor's toolbox to see how we can do this.

When Is Your Presence Present?

To expand your presence you must become aware of how you are using it. The three circles of energy is a helpful method to gauge whether you are showing up fully present in your interactions with others or if you need to 'get out of your own way' so that you can beam with more clarity.

Patsy Rodenburg, a highly-respected voice and drama coach, identifies three basic ways human energy moves in her book *Presence*. These circles of energy help performers craft their presence on stage. You too can use this knowledge to bring awareness to how you are using your energy in your interactions on your sacred stage.

Take a look at the following circles of energy. We can move through all three of these energy circles very rapidly and need to use all three at different times in our lives, but second circle energy is the energy space where your presence is fully visible.

First Circle Energy:

In today's distracted and tech-driven world, you will easily be able to identify this circle of energy. We enter this energy state when we are preoccupied with ourselves; our energy is directed inward, we come across as withdrawn and speak to others as if we are talking to ourselves. We come into this state when we feel victimised and our body posture sinks inwards. This energy state is becoming more and more common. Our habitual use of mobile phones and busy lifestyles create this inward 'half-hearted' focus. It's hard work being around someone in this state because they give very little of themselves.

Third Circle Energy:

This is the opposite to first circle energy. The energy is pushed outward with force alongside the body posture, but is not directed. There is no space for connection with this energy interaction and someone using it may come across as arrogant and speak over you. It's controlling and superficial. A typical scenario would be someone who walks into a room and starts to speak loudly, although they aren't speaking to anyone in particular. They are heard, but no one listens to them – their energy is going out in a generalised push. This is a great example of really bad acting!

Second Circle Energy:

This is when you are 'fully present' so that your unique presence can be seen. It's charismatic and magnetic in quality and it's something an actor works to be continually in performance. In this state, you are centred, aware, lively and connected to the energy both inside and outside of you. Your sense of space widens as does your peripheral vision. The volume and intonation of your voice will move with the energy flow of the conversation you're having. You become conscious of your physical actions and how they are being conveyed to your audience. This state is the place to be if you want to get to know yourself. This state breeds intimacy and equality and you can communicate with others effectively. Also, when you are in this energy state, you are an open channel and are able to gather and receive the inspirational energy of your co-creator and transmit the beauty of your soul. This is your place of power.

Try this simple exercise to bring yourself into second circle energy:

Second Circle Energy Exercise

Step 1:
Firstly, stand upright with your legs slightly apart, shoulders

back, and chest expanded. Hold your arms out in front of your chest in a relaxed fashion and imagine your heart opening. Next, bring your awareness to your breath and breathe deeply – when you are conscious of your breath your consciousness is brought into the present moment. Ask yourself: *"Am I still breathing?"* And observe the answer. This should be enough to bring you into second circle energy.

Sometimes our energy is scattered and needs calling back to us. If you are not feeling your 'lively' presence do step two before moving to step three.

Step 2:
Call back your energy. Connect with a focus outside of yourself to create a two-way energy flow. Open your eyes wide and imagine you are wearing a big white wedding dress that goes on for miles. At the end of the wedding dress is your 'lively' energy; focus on this with your eyes and invite it to come to you, and gather it into a ball with your hands. Hold your hands in front of your abdomen and feel the energy accumulating. After some time, you will start to feel heat and a tingly sensation – there will be a substantial quality to the gathering energy. Once you have accumulated enough energy, slowly move your hands down to just below your navel; bringing them closer to your body as you travel downwards. Image you are absorbing the ball of 'lively' light energy into your Dan Tien – this is your core energy centre – your 'sea of chi'.

Step 3:
Move your body – you will feel light, alert and receptive. Next, play with and explore your energy presence. Remember in Chapter 3 we talked about 'feeling into' the other to understand their energy? That is what you can do here. For example, if you are reading a book, connect with the texture and colour of its cover, project your energy and invite its energy to interact with

you, use your senses to feel the energy behind the words. Listen to it, get curious with what it has to say and what you can learn from it.

This is the perfect energy space to be in if you want to connect intimately with anyone. Try it on a date!

The Theatre of Soul

The Director's Chair – Your Soul's Seat

You have a story of greatness to tell and your soul is your director, guiding you to tell it in the most authentic, believable way possible. Your soul is the perfect director; challenging, patient, kind; it acknowledges your vulnerability and has empathy for it. And it never gives up on you. If you let your soul lead it will guide you to a place where you can come to life and create magic.

With your soul in the director's chair you will start to see your place on Earth's sacred stage is essential and your uniqueness invaluable. Only you can offer your gifts to the world, only you can bring your unique expression, only you can share your story. You understand how you are adding to the development of humanity and the planet, which brings a sense of purpose in all you do.

How To Follow the Direction of Your Soul

Hearing the direction of your soul is usually very simple, but following it can be challenging. Where we go wrong, like so many actors, is that we 'think' we know best and, like Hamlet, we get caught up in our structured lives by wanting to do the 'right thing'. It then becomes 'normal' to follow the direction of our unsupervised mind.

Do you remember the film *The Truman Show* starring Jim Carrey? Truman, the main character, was adopted by a TV company and has starred in his own reality TV show since birth. He had no idea that this was happening, and everyone around him tries in desperation to stop him from discovering the truth – that he is living an artificial existence. At the end of the film he sails off in a boat to discover his truth. "They" try to convince him to stay, saying that there is no more truth out there and that he will be safe in his artificial world. He chooses to continue and listens to the inner nudges of his soul, eventually his boat punctures the wall of the TV studio and he finds an exit door.

Like Truman we must have the courage to sail through our illusions to get curious and go beyond what we know to discover our truth.

Let's look at how we can do this.

The Fourth Wall

In the theatre, we have a term called 'the fourth wall'. This traditional theatre convention is the imaginary wall that exists between actors on stage and the audience. The audience can see through this wall, but the actors act as if they cannot. Of course, no wall actually exists, but the 'agreement' between the audience and the actors to pretend it does holds the illusion of theatre in place; they 'suspend disbelief' for a time, to make the performance seem natural and normal. The actors can do their job in safety without any interruption and the audience can be entertained without having to do anything.

The trouble with this agreement is that the audience are left passive and have no responsibility or control over the performance, which can lead to them not caring what happens to the characters and even a few snores! Without an audience there is no theatre – there is no sacred reflection of life – we need attentive audiences who actively participate. This is very much like life.

Understanding Your Fourth Wall

When we don't heed the direction of our soul we, too, develop a fourth wall. We live only in the front stage area of life – this is the world you see manifesting in front of you. In this arena, you become a 'passive audience', bored with your own acting; your life becomes limited, dull and predictable. Disenchantment sets in and all your actions and routines – going to work, getting the kids ready for school, calling your daughter, even sex with your partner – can lack meaning and become habitual and artificial.

Go Backstage

You also have an unseen backstage area, a chaotic quantum space where everything works behind the scenes to support the beliefs that 'you' – the passive audience – are observing from the front stage. This backstage area is a place where meaning is brought to life – it's your inner world that guides your outward actions. When you connect with your soul it breaks through the imaginary wall and leads you into your empowering backstage. This is the place you can come to change, rest, rehearse and understand the workings of your life.

If you want to make changes in your life or leave your 'conventional' stage completely, you'll need to smash through the fourth wall that exists in your mind and watch the illusions shatter to the ground. When you break through your fourth wall you will come to see your entire theatre production in action. This will bring meaning to your life and reinstate the harmonious relationship between your mind, body and soul.

We are the audience of our lives and whatever we believe about our front stage area, the backstage area will work to support that. We are also the actors of our lives; we can choose to follow the direction of our soul.

How To Smash through Your Fourth Wall

Interact with Yourself:
Keep the relationship open between 'you' the actor and 'you' the audience – interact. Observe yourself in action and communicate feedback. Heckle yourself! 'Freeze' the show if you must, get up on your stage and show the actor how to make the changes necessary for an authentic and awe-inspiring performance. This dual position is liberating and creates an empowering energy flow that stops you reacting to your life. You also stop projecting and transferring your own desire to take action onto other people or things. Make this a habit and your awareness will increase.

Go Backstage Daily:
Backstage is your unseen, infinite world. Your co-creator, spirit guides, shadows, angels, archetypes and soul directors all hang out here. Use their expertise and ask for help. They will show you reason and meaning behind everything that is, was and is yet to come. Go here daily to keep all your channels of communication open and clear. Take time to be silent and still, to listen to your authentic core and observe how and why you are making meaning.

Take Pleasure in Your Routines:
Get curious about every action you make. You can do this by staying present and coming into second circle energy. This makes even the most mundane chores seem adventurous.

Don't Take Yourself Too Seriously:
Bring a sense of play to your world. Laugh! Comedy can bring balance to even the darkest of situations. We are often as predictable as a pantomime with our habits and behaviours. We, the audience, know exactly what's going to happen and we sit back and let it happen anyway. Then we wonder why we did that again! Next time you feel this interrupt the show – try shouting to yourself: "He's behind you," or "Oh, yes you can!"

Act on Direction:
Your soul directs you through the use of signs, symbols and images – it has a vision for you. As a director, your soul will guide you with intuitive nudges, gut instincts, synchronicities and coincidences – respond to them and listen intently to your feelings. You can trust and believe in this direction. Once you do, your backstage crew will be busily organising that belief to come true.

Chapter 7

The Living Bridge of Pattern

Let's paint a picture....

The Day Alice Met the Baker's Son

Once upon a time there was a good girl called Alice. Every morning, without fail, Alice would kick off her muddy boots, knock twice on the door of her father's office, wait for his reply, walk in quietly, and sit upright on the large leather chair opposite his desk.

Her father would respond by squinting, standing up, and listing her chores for the day.

Alice would listen attentively, thank her father, and leave the room.

This morning ritual was repeated for many, many years and shaped the life of Alice. She was always prompt for her early morning meeting with her father, which meant a strict bedtime curfew of 8pm.

One glorious sunny afternoon, Alice was running her errands in the local village and bumped into Tom the baker's son. He was a handsome lad with arms of steel. Alice stepped into the road and literally knocked him off his bike, tipping the fresh bread everywhere!

"Oy!" he exclaimed. Alice apologised profusely, gathering French loaves with one hand and mopping his flustered brow with the hem of her skirt with the other.

Time paused for a moment. Their eyes locked and it was love at first sight. Tom took Alice for a pint of cider and they discovered how much they had in common; they both drank cider, they both loved to ride bikes, and they were both the same age. Tom wove a corn dolly for Alice and gave it to her as a gift.

Alice forgot all about the time and arrived home at 10pm.

The next morning, Alice woke with a dreamy smile, until she looked at the clock. She was late for her meeting.

She panicked and ran as fast as she could. She burst into her father's office and sat on his desk panting, as her muddy boots dangled beneath her.

"I'm so sorry I'm late, Father," she said.

Her father squinted and stood up as usual, but this time he actually saw Alice for the first time in years. His eyes welled with tears at the sight of his beautiful daughter and he said, "My darling, Alice. Look what a beautiful strong woman you have become. It's time to find you a husband."

Patterns create lives, let's explore yours.

What Does the Living Bridge of Pattern Offer the Life Artist?

As we step onto the Living Bridge of Pattern, we sink deeply into the boggy core of creation and discover the foundation of all life. Rest for a while on this sprawling bridge; trust Mother Earth to hold you steady in your unfolding. You are supported. With each step the vines of unity and balance will bestow their blessings of peace upon you, as you expand with insight.

In this chapter, you will have an opportunity to explore the power of your pattern – to reach in and pull out insight and potential. You have patterns everywhere – from your imprint in the star-studded mosaic right down to your individual fingerprints. The mystery of life is contained in your pattern. Knowing your physical, mental and spiritual energy patterns unlocks your ability to make practical use of them; to achieve your full potential and become a conscious co-creator.

What Are Patterns?

The flower of life is the name for the pattern that is found in all living things, you included. It is a template for life itself. All patterns are essentially blueprints of energy; they are the dance of consciousness, bringing life to our meaning and meaning to our lives. The way we choose to express these energy blueprints form the very root systems of our lives.

How Do We Create Patterns?

To answer this question let's head back to our sacred stage for a moment. Everything in the theatre is brought to life with a pattern: the costumes, the dance, the dialogue, the music and the lighting. These patterns are brought to life by a repetitive rehearsal system consisting of space, time, rhythm and sequence. This system brings order and meaning to the chaos of the stage and it highlights the relationship between all things, revealing how they are connected. We all know what we should be doing, when it should happen and who should be doing what. Harmony reigns!

Just like the theatre, we use pattern to bring order and meaning to our lives. The patterns that you have in place create your life and have an impact on who you are. By exploring the power of your pattern, you will understand the relationships between all areas of your life and how you are creating meaning between them. You'll be able to see the fruit of your life, nurture new buds and pluck out the rotten ones.

How Do We Unlock the Potential Held in Our Patterns?

We look at them! We already know from Part One of the book that we are pattern-seekers – it's in our DNA. We also know that when we look with our eagle's eye and 'shed light' on something, we alter our relationship to it. The simple act of looking at our patterns will help us to know them and unlock hidden insight.

If we want to expand our vibrational frequency and unlock our potential we must look at the underlying patterns running the show.

Let's get started...

The Pattern of Mind

What Brings Your Mind To Life?

"Make your mind up!" Many of us use that phrase and it means hurry up and make a decision one way or another. What if we take it more literally… how do we make our minds up? How do we bring them to life?

Drawing on the work of Freud, psychologist Carl Jung identified three parts that make up the mind:

- your conscious mind – this is your will, your here-and-now awareness.
- your subconscious mind, which controls things like your breathing, instincts, heartbeat, beliefs, emotions.
- your unconscious mind, which houses both your personal unconscious – all the information that is present in your mind, but not easily available to consciously recall such as: memories you have suppressed – and the collective unconscious, which is an inherited collection of experiences shared with the rest of humanity.

Think of them as an iceberg, the tip that we can see is the conscious mind, the others lie hidden.

Together your minds work as a team bringing your body, soul and mind to life with the constant replication of patterns. When these patterns are used frequently they form our mindsets.

Mindsets

Is your mind set for life?

A 'mindset' happens when the chaotic energy whirling between our minds is set into a pattern via repetitive use of our neural pathways; they act like pencils, continually defining you.

These are formed from a variety of things, including your social, cultural, and educational experience and your ancestral and morphic energy fields.

Think of a mindset as a map of energy carved out by the knife of your beliefs, judgments, images and attitudes. The more we use this map the stronger and more defined it becomes.

It's important to get to know our maps because they guide our thoughts and actions, which create our lives. They also influence our energy vibration. This is a two-way relationship – our energy vibe also influences and shapes our mindset. This is great news because it means that we are not 'set for life', we can change our maps, sail into our uncharted waters, and discover our exotic lands. We just need to know how to create the best maps for us!

What we see in our lives has a lot to do with how we see it.

Your mindsets decide what you see, they produce your images. We use our mindsets like a camera lens and attach them to experience life in a particular way – it's the way we perceive, organise and interpret information. And just like a camera lens, they filter out information to create your 'frame of mind', shaping the way you see yourself and the world around you. This, in turn, shapes the way you do things, which influences your energy, which influences your mindset and so on! Yes, it's cyclical!

If we want to reshape our mindsets we first need to know what shape they are in to start with.

What Shape Is Your Mindset in?

The difference between us seeing or not seeing our potential is largely due to our mindset.

A simple way to look at how our mindsets shape our meaning is with the classic example – 'Is your glass half full or half empty?'

Some people might look at the glass and see it as half empty. Their mindset is focused on what is lacking. This is often considered pessimistic because it limits their ability to see all they do have.

Some choose the opposite and say it's half full. This is considered optimistic – there is still water available to drink. Their meaning is created from what they have and leads to appreciation and gratitude.

And some might say: it's completely full – it's full of what I can see, in this case water, and what I can't see – air. This mindset is a great one for us to use because it's expanding. As Life Artists, it helps us to see the infinite space we have available to work with – both known and unknown – allowing the unseen to float into our awareness. This mindset is how you can spot your potential propping up the bar!

What Makes Us Choose One Mindset over Another?

Any photographer will tell you that they have a favourite lens; mine is my telephoto. I can capture details from a distance and feel intimate with my wildlife subjects. I can depend on it to deliver sharp results and create high quality images. However, it has its limits. If I want to capture a sweeping landscape scene, this close-up won't cut it. I need to shift to a wide angle.

Similarly, with our mindsets we tend to have favourites and use ones that have delivered great results before. When I do the weekly shop, for example, I'll 'gear myself up' and attach my efficient supermarket shopping lens. With this lens, I'll know the best time to go, the best place to park, I can whizz around each aisle with my inbuilt GPS supermarket map, finding each item on my list quickly and be in and out in an hour. I'll put the shopping away and take off the lens until next week. This is a great mindset for getting my shopping done quickly, but it does have its limits.

Sometimes, I expand my range. I'll take my time and glide

around the clothing section, or linger in the magazine aisle. I tend to have a more pleasurable experience, although I usually end up with items not on my list!

All mindsets have limits because they filter out information, but what happens when they start filtering out the authentic you?

Mindsets are not necessarily good or bad – they are either useful or not. It's easy to get stuck in a boggy mindset. This happens when we are using our favourite one too often or forget we are using them. We stop extending our vision or drawing new maps and our mindset becomes fixed.

When our mindsets are fixed, we start to crop and prune our vision of life to look like the one in our mind. We try to control our roots, we domesticate them and, alongside them, some of our spirit.

Is Your Mindset Fixed?

Your mindset determines what you believe about yourself. If your mindset becomes fixed you can start to believe your ability is innate – there is nothing you can do to change your situation. This ignites the fear of failure and victimhood, which can be devastating; it makes you doubt how good you are, stop believing in yourself and stop trying. Eventually you start to measure yourself by your failures, rather than believing you can improve your situation or your ability and keep growing.

As human beings we naturally have an expanding pattern. We are 'flowers of life', which is why, when we stop growing, we feel as though something is missing or see less of ourselves.

If this sounds like you, a simple way to unfix your mindset is by clearing your energy system daily.

Try the following energy routine to keep your pattern beautiful.

How to Clear the Energy of a Mindset

Start the day in a beautiful way: cleanse, tone and moisturise

Tip: Slip the following two-minute routine alongside a powerful daily habit like showering, cleaning your teeth or going to the toilet. Choose somewhere where you can have privacy and won't be disturbed. The toilet or shower is especially beneficial because your physical body is also being cleansed alongside your energetic body. Do the routine as many times a day as possible – no less than twice – and you will begin to purify your vibrational frequency and start to notice a difference straight away.

Cleanse:

- Take a couple of deep breaths and 'feel into' yourself.
- Next, set your focus and intent to clear your energy system. In your mind's eye say to yourself: "My energy is clear."
- Imagine all the stagnant, murky energy draining out of your feet and into the earth. Or down the plughole or toilet, depending on where you are.

Tone:

- Drop into second circle energy and bring your full awareness to the sea of chi energy found just below your navel – your 'dan tien'. Feel your presence expand as you breathe, and centre yourself.
- Next, bring your expanded awareness to your heart and allow the energy of love to grow and spread throughout your body. Truly feel it. This energy is shifting and lightening your vibration. If you find it difficult to feel this energy, think of a beautiful memory that is filled with love energy as a starting point. Then deliberately increase

the intensity of the energy keeping it alive for as long as you can. Imagine it filling your body from head to toe and oozing from every pore.

Moisturise:

- Consciously allow this energy to seep into your actions and soften your mindset: hold your pen, glass, talk, walk, write, look with the loving, nurturing energy for as long as possible.

You will see from the energy routine above that our mind influences our body and our body also influences our mind. This is a fundamental relationship to explore if we wish to gain deeper insights into our core pattern – our place in the star-studded mosaic.

Let's take a closer look at the mind-body body-mind connection.

The Pattern of Body

What's your relationship like with your body?

Embedded in our bodies are destiny maps, ancestral maps, magical maps, health maps – you have a plethora of wisdom stored in your thighs. Your body is an intelligent powerhouse and the greatest healer you know.

Why don't we use this wisdom more?

Relationship Status – It's Complicated

As women, we deny ourselves access to our store of wisdom because of our complicated relationship with our bodies. I know very few women who have a deeply satisfying and loving relationship with their bodies. Instead, we tend to look at ourselves in parts – face, hip, bum, breasts – we literally pick ourselves to bits! The pressure a woman feels to look the 'most beautiful' gets in the way of her discovering her powerful and beautiful wisdom.

I am no exception. I have had a turbulent relationship with my body from a very early age. In fact, I can't ever remember loving it deeply and unconditionally. At best, I liked parts of it. My menstrual cycle started at the age of ten and I blamed my body yet again for making me feel different and separated from the others in my class at primary school. But, it wasn't until I was fourteen and diagnosed with epilepsy that a deep distrust set in and started to rot my roots.

Do You Trust Your Body?

Epilepsy is a very misunderstood and mysterious condition. It has been called the "falling sickness" or "sacred disease". Centuries ago I would have been regarded as demonically possessed, locked up in a mental institution or rounded up with the witches and burnt. In the early 1980s my response was to enter denial and ignore it. Secretly, I blamed and shamed my body.

I was determined not to let "the sacred disease" define me or stop me from doing anything. I held down a challenging job, I drove a car, I performed on stage, I skydived, I travelled the world alone, I lived alone. Denying its existence had served me well. Of course, I am blessed compared to some who typically have three seizures a day and are unable to control them. But controlled or not, tucked away in the depths of my mind is the constant threat of attack. It lies sleeping like an angry dragon that I have been forced to notice and respect.

The truth is I can monitor my triggers, but I have no conscious control if or when the dragon decides to strike. And when it does I have no warning – it swallows me violently; my consciousness leaves my body with the first bite. There is nothing romantic or mystical about it for me; unlike the Russian writer Dostoevsky, I don't have the temporal lobe type of epilepsy that brings impressions or makes me feel such bliss before the storm that I am "imbued with God". I wish I felt that – it would bring some reason to this destructive force. I do sense that when my consciousness leaves my body it goes to a beautiful place where I could happily stay.

When the seizure ends, I arrive back in my body stripped of ego. I am childlike, loving and gentle – so I've been told. Exhausted, I have to sleep. After some time, I awake and I'm fully present in my body. This is the torturous part – slowly waking and sensing something is wrong. A feeling of dread satiates me and I'm flung into victim mode. Why am I being punished again? The agony of memory loss stabbing at my brain brings with it the familiar knowing. A dark cloud of despair descends, and when it finally dawns on me what has happened, the dread is replaced by profound sorrow. "Why?"

Next, follows complete and total body pain unique to a seizure;

it feels as though every single part of me has been devoured, chewed, and spat back out. It takes a good couple of days for me to put the pieces of my scattered energy back together again. Scattered energy can leave people feeling very strange after a seizure, often as if they are not 'fully themselves'. To integrate and ground my energy, I've found it helps if I immerse my body in a warm bath and then do a meditation to consciously call back all my energy parts and strengthen my aura.

We don't need to have epilepsy to develop a deep distrust of our body; any type of illness – from chronic autoimmune disorders to cancer – can shock us, sever our connection, and alter the relationship we have with our body. The good news is that this can be repaired if we look for lessons and gently listen to and understand her immense wisdom.

How To Begin Trusting Your Body

My understanding of the mind-body connection deepened when I started working with energy and experienced my first-degree reiki attunement. It was here that I also learnt to accept, trust and listen to the wisdom held in my body. After I received my attunement I floated back to my room and drifted gently to sleep. It was that evening that a trauma buried in the darkest tunnels of my unconscious flew into my awareness. Like a phoenix, I was finally set free from my energetic bindings.

If you don't know the story of the phoenix, it's a mythical bird that consciously consumes itself in flames to be reborn anew from its ashes. It symbolises the transformation of human consciousness. Something within me changed forever that evening; I flew so close to the light of my sun that the deep wounds I had no idea I'd been harbouring could rise to the surface to be seen, integrated and healed, and I started to appreciate the wisdom of my body.

It's extraordinary how brave and intelligent our bodies actually are. I learnt how my mind and body worked together to protect me from feeling the pain of trauma; they found a way for me to escape. I realised I had been blaming my body, and therefore myself, for everything that happened to me as a little girl. I also learnt that, if I was to shift my consciousness, I needed to accept and listen to my wisdom, by integrating the energy patterns embedded in my body.

What if our bodies are not a problem to solve?

Finally, I realised that my body is not a problem to solve – it is a guide to listen to. This is the first step to reconnecting with your body wisdom. Take responsibility for your body and accept it exactly as it is – every breath, scar, hair and stretchmark. Quit measuring yourself against something that you are not and give your body a chance to be who you are. Quit telling it it's not good enough and shaming it. Quit pressuring it; making it your entire world and responsible for your happiness. Love it day by day, respond to its needs and you'll learn to harness your body's unique healing force and wisdom.

How To Begin Listening To Your Body

Just breathe.

How annoying is it when you are stressed out and someone says those words to you? It's irritating because you know they are so right! Your breath is your natural sedative when you are angry, your natural energiser when you are tired, your natural comforter when you are sad. You can create and control your emotions by changing your breathing pattern. The next time you feel angry, try breathing slowly and deeply and watch yourself relax. We often forget about or underestimate the power of our breath; it truly is the source of our life here on Earth. It aids digestion, oxygenates your blood, revitalises the life of every single cell you possess, disrupts limiting mindsets and body patterns, and unites your mind, body and soul so that you can hear your truth and co-create with spirit. It's an essential tool for a 'life' artist!

Our breath literally fills us with spirit and keeps us healthy, so why is it that most of us don't automatically breathe to our full lung capacity? We are born breathing naturally, but over the years our lifestyles shape our bodies and we simply forget! Many of us have fallen into habits of shallow breathing, anxious breathing, or even holding our breath. All of these tense our body and restrict our natural energetic power. Rarely do we breathe from our diaphragm; instead many of us breathe from the chest, which restrains both our life force and our senses. I first became aware of my shallow breathing when I started to sing and work with my voice. I learnt to increase my lung capacity by consciously breathing correctly and practising breathing techniques.

If you want to enter the wisdom held in your body you can become aware of your breathing patterns and adapt them accordingly. Yoga has a wealth of breathing exercises called Pranayama, all of them designed to intensify your life force. When you relearn to breathe naturally, your life force moves freely throughout your body and your truth can be felt and seen.

Your breath is the access point to listening to your body. Practise the simple exercise below to develop the habit of proper breathing and listening to your body.

Breathe and Listen Exercise

- Inhale through the nose: Place one hand on your upper chest and the other just below your ribcage; take a deep breath and feel your diaphragm rise beneath your hands, pushing them upwards.
- Exhale slowly through the mouth, pursing your lips. Feel

this breath move through your entire body, relaxing it as it passes through. Listen with your full awareness.

Repeat this for about ten minutes or until you feel connected with your body.

When you feel the connection, 'feel into' and dialogue with your body and listen to how it responds. It will help you to feel what is real and true for you. Note down any impressions and information in a journal.

The Pattern of Soul

In the previous chapter, we explored our soul as director. The reason why your soul knows how and where to direct you is because it carries the imprint and intent of both spirit and your mind-body consciousness in its energy pattern. Your soul is your link to your co-creator. And it not only contains information from your experience in this lifetime, but all the lifetimes you have experienced. Your soul holds a wealth of wisdom about you.

Soul Lessons

Let's head back to the star-studded mosaic for a moment to remind ourselves of our soul's role in our pattern. Your soul has the job of aligning the pattern of your body-mind consciousness with your spirit's desire, so that you can express your purpose. Life is filled with value, meaning and beauty when you express this direction – it becomes your art. Life flows. We learn the growth lessons necessary to keep us expanding, and life, although challenging at times, becomes heart-felt and filled with love.

I'm not suggesting this leads to a Pollyanna approach to life. We will still experience challenges, pain and loss, but there is a difference between soul lessons – we need to experience these to expand – and destructive patterns of behaviour caused by fixed mind/body patterns, which we can release.

Life starts to get a bit messy and tricky when our mindsets and body patterns are taking us in one direction, and the spirit in us wants to go in another! This is when Alchemy Moments pop up, offering us the opportunity to bring our life into a greater alignment with our spirit's purpose. It's our choice.

Here we can see the importance of regularly assessing our mind and body patterns to see if they are supporting our soul's calling or hindering it.

A great practical way to explore your patterns is with the

use of mandalas. The mandala speaks your soul's language in symbols, and can help you to access the ever-expanding world that exists both within and beyond your body and mind.

The Mandala

If you remember, in Chapter 2 we looked at the power of the circle and how life is represented by it. Nature is embedded with circles; the Sun, the Moon and the Earth all remind us that we are part of the whole. We are a part of Nature and follow the same cyclical patterns.

The ancient mandala is one of the most insightful and nourishing forms you can use to relate to your patterns. The word mandala is Sanskrit and means wheel – it's a circular design that represents the universe. What's really magical about the mandala is that it can be used to contemplate your relationship to your body, your psychological state, your place in the world and absolutely anything else, from the relationship with your boss, to your past lives. It reveals and translates information about any patterns you choose and transforms life's mysteries to a scale that can be understood.

How To Use a Mandala

When I use the mandala, I follow a process like this:

Firstly, I direct my energy by setting my intent, for example – "I hear my body's wisdom I am healthy," or "To reveal my life's purpose." My intent directs my energy to the pattern I want to retrieve information from and connects them.

Next, I place myself into a neutral state, breathing deeply to connect my mind and body, and then I start the meditative process of drawing the mandala. The mandala acts like a mirror; it becomes a symbol of the energy held within me. The process of painting the mandala helps me to decode the information; it pulls me beyond the surface of what I know to see my connections, and I am imparted with insight. The end result is a beautiful pattern filled with the energetic intent that I set at the beginning, plus insight into ways that can help me achieve my intent.

Mandalas are built for balance and they can show you how to bring balance into all areas of your life. Remember they are a reflection of your pattern now, a snapshot of you in the moment, offering you a source of healing and wholeness.

The process of creating a mandala feels very natural and gentle. It lends itself to highlighting and clearing our inner conflicts, bringing harmony to our patterns. It also has the added bonus of de-stressing and relaxing you.

Try it for yourself...

How To Create a Mandala

Resources required: paper, colouring pencils, felt tips or paints, scissors.

Prepare Your Equipment:
Draw a large circle on a piece of paper, cut it out. Find the centre point by folding the paper in half and then half again. Unfold the paper and place a dot in the centre. If you want more structure for your mandala you can draw a few more circles inside it.

Prepare Yourself:
Next, take a couple of deep breaths to relax you and connect your mind and body. When you feel focused and alert, set your intent with clarity, awareness and feeling.

Make the Mandala:
Start your mandala from the centre point, spiralling outwards from the circle, in a clockwise direction. Fill it with colours, symbols and shapes that come to mind. The important thing is to *repeat your*

shapes, colours and symbols so they form a pattern. This will tend to happen naturally if you are relaxed and tuned in.

Don't get hung up on being too accurate with your symmetry; instead allow your mind to fall into a meditative state, observe yourself, take your time, and enjoy the process. This allows your mind to 'get out of your way' providing a valuable space for insights to arise. If you make a mistake, work with it – they are often blessings in disguise, showing us ways to change our pattern.

Title Your Mandala:
When you have completed the mandala take some time to observe the whole pattern. Note down your feelings and your impressions of the shapes, symbols and colours you used:

- Do they energise or relax you?
- What meaning do they hold for you?
- Are there any parts that irritate you or bring pleasure? How does this relate to the process of creation? Where do you feel these sensations in your body?
- How do the elements relate to each other?
- Is there a great amount of free space or is the design intricate and detailed?
- How do all of these characteristics relate to your intent and your life?

When you have finished interpreting your mandala, give it a title and enjoy its energy.

Chapter 8

The Living Bridge of Mask

Let's paint a picture....

The Invisible Mask

A long time ago, when myths and legends were real, there lived a miserable little girl who spent her days weeping underneath the wise willow. She sobbed so many tears that they formed an entire lake.

The great Lake God Spiritus rose up from the depths and thanked the girl for his freedom.

"My dear girl," he said. "Like a genie from the bottle, you have set me free. I now I have a duty to grant you one wish."

The girl wiped the final tear from her plain, puffy face and thought long and hard about what her wish could be. She was dreadfully upset because all the other girls were beautiful. She felt so different, and no matter how hard she searched, her beauty was nowhere to be found. Hesitantly she said to Spiritus: "I wish to be shown my beauty, to be made beautiful at last."

"Your wish is my command, but you will have to follow my instructions without question," he said. The girl agreed wholeheartedly and waited for her instructions.

"First, you must wear this invisible mask," said the Lake God. "It will protect you from the blinding light of your beauty."

The girl obediently placed the mask upon her face.

"Next, you must walk over to the edge of the lake and look into my heart. A reflection will appear. That is your beauty. You must remember to never question your beauty or it will disappear forever."

As the girl peered into the heart of the lake, she fell in love with the exquisite vision reflected back: a goddess who wore galaxies in her hair, twinkled stars from her eyes, and smiled like the moon. The little girl was overjoyed at her new-found beauty and vowed to share it across the land, bringing the light of the cosmos to all she met.

Sometimes we must remove the distorted mirrors held in our eyes to reveal the beauty that resides beyond. Let's explore how the mask can help us to do this.

What Does the Living Bridge of Mask Offer the Life Artist?

The living bridge of mask is misleading in appearance – it is more like a hall of mirrors than a bridge. As you trample upon its myriad layers, you'll discover all the faces you'll ever own and disown, together reflecting your maze of truth. I won't lie, this journey is unsettling and disorientating. It takes mighty courage to tread the contrary path of looming shadows, but the rewards are epic; you can taste your divinity and emerge a heroine.

Why are you crossing the living bridge of mask? What can it offer you? You might think it's farcical to use the art form of masking to help you to access your authentic self. After all, aren't authenticity and masking complete opposites? On first glance, this assumption seems obvious, but if we delve a little deeper into the mask, we discover that it's precisely this dualistic nature of masks that gives them their transformational quality and power. Through embodying your masks, you are able to see and integrate parts of yourself that you never knew existed.

The Power of the Mask

I love the work of Oscar Wilde. His words bottle the shadows of humanity and reveal the societal and emotional masks held by us all. He places them between perfumed pages so that we might refresh ourselves lightly with truths that are as poignant today as they were in the 1890s. When he wrote: "Give a man a mask and he'll tell you the truth," he summed up the real nature of the mask and the benefits you can gain by exploring yours – seeing, knowing and transforming your authentic truth.

These days you may only come across masks at Halloween, or if you're heading to a fancy-dress party or a summer festival. Nevertheless, you still might experience stirrings of trepidation when you hear the word mask mentioned. A mysterious and sinister reputation often precedes the mask, and although fascinated, we are usually wary of them.

I've been working and teaching with masks for many years, and they never cease to amaze me; I still marvel at their mysterious powers.

Let me share an instance with you. Many moons ago, as a drama teacher I had the opportunity to work with a group of troubled teenage boys on their 'last chance' before being excluded from school. At the age of 15 they were tough and absolutely did not want to be in my class. They thought drama was for wimps and told me so with guns blazing! The first day the group of boys turned up. Three walked in ten minutes late and one kicked a chair over; they were either defiant, reluctant, or silently evasive. I had my work cut out!

I could see that they had entered the space wearing their personal masks of protection. After the ordeal of taking the register, I knew there was no way they were going to willingly enter into the work I had planned. Or was there? I popped into the adjoining office and grabbed a box of masks. I found a sinister old hag type character – I was identifying with it quite strongly at the time! I put it on, grabbed my black scarf and threw it around my shoulders. Standing outside the classroom door I knocked three times and paused; slowly opening the door and peering creepily around it. Their response as I performed for them was delightful; after the initial shock came laughter and heckling, then an enthralled silence. I could see their protective masks melt as faces started to soften and curiosity arose. They even gave me a round of applause!

During the weeks that followed, masks provided a much-needed platform of expression for these guys. Using the performance mask gave them an opportunity to drop their protective masks and play. They were able to be children, unlock the power of their vulnerability and find a voice to say what they didn't even know they wanted to say! Masks reveal the unknown in the body, mind and spirit, they are truth magnifiers, exposing the golden glow of authenticity hidden beneath the ego.

How Do We Unlock the Power in Our Masks?

Our ancestors understood the power of the mask and used them to speak with the Gods, heal the sick and transmute evil, as well as entertain themselves. They knew how to find the spirit of the mask and use this as a portal into a unique perceptual space.

There is no doubt that masks contain a supernatural quality. Each one possesses its own spirit; they take on a persona of their own and possess the ability to conceal what is known, reveal what is unknown, and allow both to exist simultaneously. Body and mind, spiritual and earthly, light and dark, good and evil – all oppositions can be present when a mask is worn.

What is less apparent, yet significant for the Life Artist, is the space in between – where the oppositions merge. I call it "No Man's Land". This houses the true spirit of the mask, the meeting space that unites the opposing energies and releases their power. It is on this fertile ground you can experience transformation and unearth your buried treasure.

The Spirit of Your Mask

In this chapter you will have an opportunity to dig around in No Man's Land, uncover the spirit of your masks and extract the wisdom they offer you. But first you must recognise them, which is not as easy as it seems – after all, masks are masters of disguise!

Your masks are unique to you, and understanding how

you use them in your everyday lives can free you from deep-rooted patterns, unwanted behaviours and habits that stop you from expanding. Finding the spirit in your masks is extremely liberating; it stops them 'running the show' and having power 'over' you. Instead, your blinkers are removed, your eagle eye is extended and you are empowered by seeing and accepting 'all that you are'.

Let's start by recognising the two fundamental elements masks need for their spirits to emerge.

1. The Masquerade

The very nature of the masquerade involves disguising and transforming identities, revealing what lies beyond. We know that behind every illusion stands a truth, but often the truth cannot be seen without the illusion present. For the spirit of the mask to emerge, there must be a disguise – a Masquerade presenting a duality of reality and fantasy. A great example of this is the elaborate Carnival in Venice where everybody agrees to disguise themselves; they literally become works of art by adorning exquisite masks and costumes, dancing and parading their beauty. The people beneath the masks essentially fade into one as the spirit of their masks comes out to play.

The 'play' of the masquerade offers us new ways to look at our lives. We can question our reality, choose what to believe, and most of all, enjoy the playful beauty of being alive! When we recognise the masquerades of our own life we experience 'revelations'; these insights bring us awareness and lead us towards unity and wholeness.

Do you know what lies beneath the mask of your life? How does the spirit of your life mask reveal itself? If you take it off what will you see?

2. The Audience

In the theatre, hours of practice, skill and sweat go into creating a masked character. The actor is extremely dedicated to her craft – it's physically demanding work. And all of this effort is for one purpose only – an audience.

The actor's job is to make the audience 'suspend their disbelief', to want to 'see' only the masked character and not the person performing behind the mask. She wants them to believe in the character of the mask because it can reflect insight and provide revelations about their own lives. The audience gives life to the performance and permission to the mask with their belief – there is simply no masquerade without them.

We, too, innately understand the importance of the audience; we are continually involved in the masquerade and upkeep of our identity. We apply a huge amount of dedication, managing how we are appearing and what impressions we are having on others; from our speech and dress, to the car we drive, the home we live in, and the places we hang out. We have become highly skilled at displaying or disguising our identity through the use of social masks. Whole schemas of energy are embedded in the masks we wear, alongside their morphogenetic fields. They are extremely influential.

Just as the audience must believe in the illusion of the mask for it to have an impact upon them, the masks we wear in daily life are also given their power through our belief. It's how we form and transform our identities.

When you recognise the masks you wear, for what they are – masks – you instantly break through the illusion, their initial power subsides, and you can choose to use your newly-found revelations to support your growth.

What You Need To Know Before Working with Masks

Whose Face Are You Wearing?

If you've ever watched a performance using masks, you'll know they have a wonderful ability to increase empathy. The audience starts to mirror them. You will probably notice this is the same for you in your life and the people who you spend time with. After a while, you begin to unconsciously mirror them because it helps you get along with each other and builds rapport.

You might adopt their facial positions, their tone of voice and postures – you literally 'make a mask' of them to understand them further. This mirroring also happens naturally between couples; they often start to look alike, as do some dog owners with their pooches! When you recognise the masks you and others wear, your empathy and compassion will increase.

It's important to be aware of who you spend time with, and how you're shaped by them. This awareness stops you confusing the mask you made of them as yours and reminds you to remove it. You can do this by knowing your neutral position.

Know Your Neutral

In the theatre, to prepare for wearing a mask we always start from a position of neutral. This is: legs slightly apart, weight evenly distributed on both hips, neck straight, shoulders back and relaxed. This position helps you to find your centre point and be fully present.

There is even a neutral mask to work with before adopting a character mask; this helps the actor to 'reset' themselves so they can fill up with a new character and not bring any of their own idiosyncrasies to it. It allows the actor to experience a state of pure presence in the moment because the neutral mask has no memory and no dramatic expression; the actor can uncover the most efficient movement state for their space.

Knowing your neutral is really beneficial because neutral

position helps you to understand what is authentic or inauthentic for you. You will be able to identify and remove what masks you have been wearing – consciously or unconsciously – by always coming to a state of neutral. Being present and fully aware in the moment is your point of power.

TOP TIP:
Whenever you work with any masks – performance masks, social masks, yours or other people's – ask yourself the following questions to understand its intent:

What is it concealing?
What is it revealing?
What is it transforming?
What is it uniting?

The answers to these questions will help you get behind the mask and understand its true spirit.

Let's get started...

The Mask of Mind

The Two Masks of Creativity

Two masks for the Life Artist to become intimate with are the mask of the critic and the mask of the child; understanding both of these is essential to creating a fulfilling and creative life. They house powerful energies that can either hinder your creative process or support it. When you tap into their spirits you have access to life-changing qualities; they contain wise and inspirational essences that you can learn to extract and use to create your vision of beauty.

When we do anything creative the first mask we undoubtedly come into contact with is the mask of our mind – our inner critic. Let's take a look at how you can use the critic to support you.

The Critic – An Inside Job

Who Is the Critic?

Disfigured since birth, the bitter critic mask appears from the gloomiest depths of your mind. Cloaked in rejection, judgment, suppression, pressure and anxiety, its energy reeks of ageing wounds. Pretending to be your voice of authority, it spouts critical monologues, hypnotising you to be attentive, obedient and willing. Its intent is to keep you safe and secure and it does this by convincing you to believe in it and embody it.

How Is the Critic Formed?

We all wear the mask of the critic and just like any mask it has the ability to conceal, reveal, transform and unite us. Our self-esteem and self-image are developed by how we talk to ourselves. All of us have conscious and unconscious memories of all the times we felt bad or wrong – they are unavoidable scars of childhood.

The critic's voice is formed from your wounded child's defences, which are unique to you. Imagine all the traumas, hurts, rejections, negative feelings and painful memories you experienced as a child, layered into one mighty defensive mask. This is the formidable energy of the critic. And because we all have one, the morphogenic field of the critic is seriously strong; its archetypal and is part of our collective unconscious.

How To Spot Your Critic

You would expect this monstrous character to be easily identifiable, but it has been with you since childhood and it's the chameleon of disguise.

Here are a few ways to spot it:

- It regularly appears in your creative process with the overall aim to protect you and keep you safe and secure. It fears change and vulnerability.
- Your sight becomes perceptually and physically narrowed and shortened. You are blinded from your potential and refuse to find solutions to your fears. The critic knows best.
- If you notice the words "can't, don't, should" used frequently, then the critic is around. You are listening to a sprawling critical monologue inside your head: "You can't trust him, he'll reject you"; "You don't deserve to be loved"; "You should do it like that". Your physical body responds to the words and becomes limited, restricted, hunched, tired and weighed down.
- You stop doing things because you: want to fit in, don't want to look silly, or feel a failure.
- You lack compassion for yourself and/or others.
- You feel a victim, crave pity and are 'hard done by'.

The powerful energy of the inner critic is immense and drives our destructive and self-sabotaging patterns. It believes it does this for our own good. Once upon a time this coping mechanism helped us deal with pain, but as adults these defences are outdated and wreak havoc in our lives.

To reshape the old negative patterns, we must gain an understanding of the 'defence masquerades' we formed as a child; we can seek to discover the truth behind the illusion. You can do this by unmasking your critic's purpose and making your critic an ally.

How the Critic Can Work for You

When we understand how the inner critic works in us, we know ourselves better. We're able to make conscious, informed decisions about our lives and develop healthy, resilient relationships. Our level of awareness increases, leaving us with new ways of seeing. There is no doubt the energy of the critic is a strong driving force in our lives, and we can harness this for our benefit; we can reshape our self-perception and understand who we truly are and what we want in our lives. The key is to extract the harmful judgment out of our observations and discern with compassion and calmness what is really going on when the critic pops up.

You can shake off the critic's crooked lies by taking new actions and challenging the thoughts that lead you to repeat the same destructive patterns, the same harmful habits, and the same unfulfilling relationships, bringing wisdom and integrity to your choices.

We have the mask of the critic for life, so transforming it into an ally by knowing and loving yourself and making your critic a discerner is the way to go.

Once your critic feels safe, it will transform into a wise friend, and you can unearth its talents. Harness its ability to be disciplined, objective and pay attention to details. With the energy of discernment driving these qualities, they become positive and supportive, allowing your life to flow creatively.

How To Turn Your Critic into the Discerner

Unmasking Your Critic

In the theatre if the actor whips their mask off in the middle of a performance, the whole thing is ruined because the audience no longer believes in the mask – the illusion is broken. Unmasking the critic works on the same principle.

This process involves three steps:

Step 1: Notice and Observe Your Critic

To exist, the critic needs you to believe in it. To break your belief, you must closely observe the critic – get inside its head instead of it being inside yours! This close observation will loosen the formidable pull of its energetic pattern. One powerful way to do this is to literally make a mask of it. You can cut out a paper mask or buy a blank mask as your starting point. Next, draw, paint or decorate the mask until it resembles your critic. Once you've made your mask follow these mask rules to put it on and embody its character:

- Stand in a neutral position – legs slightly apart, weight evenly distributed on both hips and find your centre point.
- Make the facial expression of the mask on your face.
- Let this expression fill your body – make the body posture for your mask.
- Put the mask on your face and adjust your hair to cover the sides. Adjust your body posture again to embody the character fully.
- Stand in front of a mirror and watch yourself in the mask. Experiment with moving; notice your thoughts and feelings and its impact on your presence.
-

Step 2: Unmask Its Purpose
While you are still wearing your mask challenge the character you've embodied with compassion. Smash through your fourth wall – dialogue with your critic – heckle, talk back and reassure it that it's safe.

Use the following questions to guide you:

What is my critic concealing?
When you have your answer, pause and allow the feeling of compassion to build throughout your body. Next, write down your answer.
What is my critic revealing?
When you have your answer, pause and allow the feeling of compassion to build throughout your body. Next, write down your answer.
What is my critic transforming?
When you have your answer, pause and allow the feeling of compassion to build throughout your body. Next, write down your answer.
What is my critic uniting?
When you have your answer, pause and allow the feeling of compassion to build throughout your body. Next, write down your answer.

Step 3: Reset the Energy
Slowly remove the mask from your face, whilst watching yourself in the mirror. Next, move your body and shake out the energy. Then adopt a conscious posture; take the neutral position. Breathe deeply and centre yourself.

Reflect: How did the Critic make you feel? What effect did it have upon your body? Will you be able to recognise it the next time it pops up? *Ask yourself: What Truth Lies Behind the Mask of My Critic?*

Does the voice of your critic refuse to stop, no matter what?

You will notice as you start to go beyond the mask of your critic a familiar face appears. There is an intrinsic relationship between our inner critic and our inner child.

The Mask of Body

The Inner Child

We all have an inner child in us and it's the age of every child we've ever been. It's also every emotion and experience we've felt – innocent, abandoned, playful, magical, rejected, worthless, happy – which makes it a compelling presence. Within you, you have a playful child, an innocent child, a wounded child, an abandoned child, a magical child and so on. Your inner child is an accumulation of them all. A simple way to understand it is in terms of energy; it's the emotional, spiritual and physical energy of your childhood that you carry with you. The child is also an archetypal energy, so as well as being part of your individual psyche, the collective energy also gets thrown into the melting pot when you explore your inner child.

The Relationship Between the Critic and Child

In the previous chapter, we touched upon the interrelationship between our minds and bodies; we know that our minds can affect how healthy our bodies are and vice versa. The critic/child relationship is a prime example of this. Although you experience the critic's harsh performance in your mind, its driving force resides in your body because it is the mask of your wounded child.

The See-Saw Effect

The more traumatised, abused, neglected, and criticised you felt as a child, the louder, more dominant and overbearing your inner critic's voice is. I like to imagine them on a see-saw together; as one feels down, the other goes up. When your wounded child feels flawed and defective she covers up her true self with the critic, which is ignited in the body and is triggered by feelings of vulnerability and fear.

The critic rises up to protect us from feeling shame, unloved, unseen, unheard, neglected and worthless, all those feelings we felt as a child when we did anything bad or wrong. We all have a wounded child in us and it feels all these negative emotions once again when our harsh critical voice is in action. And so our pain is perpetuated, even though we are now adults. These critical words make us suppress the child in us further, so we play the role of the critical grown-up and choose the safe and sensible options. We deny the innocent, creative and magical qualities that the inner child holds. It's a continuous cycle.

Happy Childhood Versus Unhappy Childhood

Even if you had a happy, healthy childhood where your needs were met and you felt happy, secure and loved, you will still experience the energy of a wounded child – we all do. You may have been able to grieve and recover from those wounds and accept them as part of you, integrating them into your energetic body, which would leave you feeling connected to your inner child, and able to express the child in 'you' effortlessly. As an adult, you are now able to meet your own needs and feel a deep sense of love and empathy for yourself, feel comfortable in your body, have a balanced relationship between responsibility and independence, and feel safe to express your feelings, opinions and creativity.

Still, do give the exercise below a go. The adult world has a tendency to squash our child within and they need regular playtime. I have found that my clients who grew up 'happy' benefited massively by exploring their inner child; finding answers to health issues, relationship difficulties and generally feeling a heightened sense of vitality.

If on the other hand, you experienced traumas as a child – which can be anything from feeling ignored in your large family, being left with a horrible babysitter, to physical or sexual abuse from a family member – you will have a child that needs attention and wounds that need validating and integrating into your energetic body.

For most of us, the pain we felt from these childhood experiences was unbearable, and we have buried it, along with the child, never to be seen again. By choosing not to look at the pain we felt as children, we deny that parts of ourselves exist; we neglect and disown them. These are the parts of you that have never recovered from feeling unlovable, unworthy and flawed. However, as you know energy must express itself; these 'unexpressed' parts spill out into other areas of our lives causing us to seek validation – we look for others to give us what we cannot.

The wounded child uses the mask of the critic as a way to keep itself alive and to be seen and felt by you. When you hear the voice of your critic you will feel the wounded child in your body. This is a sign that it is trying to get your attention so that you can learn how to meet your own needs and love yourself, instead of assigning those roles to people, places, and things. When we integrate these parts into our emotional, physical and spiritual body, it fills us with love for ourselves and leads us to wholeness.

The child in us unleashes our creative, intuitive and imaginative worlds. When you access your inner child, you access part of your soul.

How Can You Connect with Your Inner Child?

If you've identified with the wounded child at all, you will benefit from bringing your child out of the shadows and building a relationship with them. These heartfelt bonds form the roots to a beautiful, fulfilling and transforming life, enabling you to feel heard and complete.

Dr Lucia Capacchione developed the following technique for getting in touch with your inner child. I use it a great deal with my clients and find it an incredibly powerful and liberating way to start the integration process.

Contacting Your Inner Child

Try the following exercise to meet with your inner child:

1. Prepare your space so that you feel safe and relaxed; light some incense, play some relaxing background music and ensure you won't be disturbed. Have a pen and some paper available.
2. Breathe and bring yourself into a neutral present state.
3. Set the intent to meet with your inner child. You may find your wounded or your playful child appears. Go with whatever comes, it will be what you need at the time.
4. With your dominant writing hand write a question to your child. Here are some examples for you:

- How old are you?
- Do you want to talk with me?
- How are you feeling?
- What do you need?
- What can I do to help you feel loved?
- What can I do to help you feel happy?

5. Place the pen in your non-dominant writing hand and hold the tip to the paper ready to write the response. When you feel or hear a response from your child, write it exactly as it comes – from your child's state – and allow it stop naturally.
6. Swap hands, bring yourself back to neutral state and ask another question. Continue like this until you have asked all the questions you want to. You will find it comes to a natural close.

Once you have completed the exercise it would be a good time to revisit the questions we set at the beginning and apply them to your inner child.

- What is it concealing?
- What is it revealing?
- What is it transforming?
- What is it uniting?

Sometimes, our inner child is nowhere to be seen. She won't show herself, or if she does, she is 'untouchable'. She has become the mask of the soul.

The Mask of Soul

I first encountered my inner child when I was doing my NLP and hypnotherapy training.

This was about a year after my reiki experience, when buried trauma had risen from the depths of my subconscious to be seen and integrated. I chose to work on that incident and prepared myself to meet the four-year-old girl within.

I settled down and relaxed slowly into a deep trance. After some time, I saw a wild half-child half-beast standing at the end of a long tunnel. Her hair was white and it looked crazily backcombed, all standing on end. She was dressed in white rags, covered in dirt, and made animal sounds, refusing to speak to me. She scared me; physically, my heart was thumping and my breathing was quick-paced. I didn't want to look at this ugly, evil child. I didn't want to see this part of me. I was ashamed of her and felt guilty that she existed. I was also upset that she wouldn't speak to me and only appeared for a fleeting moment and then left.

When I came out of the trance, I felt different. The very fact that she showed herself, even for a moment, opened my heart. I could no longer deny her existence. I was overwhelmed with a feeling of strong motherly protection, and felt such relief, such grief, such anger. It was a powerful experience, but I had a lot more work to do yet.

Soul Loss

I had experienced a trauma that caused part of my soul, my vital essence, to split from my consciousness in order to survive the experience. Now, this happened when I was very young and I had no memory of it. This meant I wasn't aware of all of the destructive patterns this led to in my life, or indeed remember what it felt like to be a 'whole soul'.

Psychologists would call this disassociation. Shamans call this 'soul loss' and believe that whenever we suffer an emotional or physical trauma, a part of our soul flees to protect itself. This soul part will not come back of its own accord because it's either too frightened, is being held captive, or it doesn't know the trauma is over. The energy is trapped or frozen. This causes the person to feel as if part of themselves is missing; their creative power is denied. This means they cannot be 'fully present' because their presence has shifted out of alignment with the energetic body. It's like having a chip in your part of the mosaic and you believe this flaw is part of your design because you don't know any different. It's ugly, so, you try covering your flaw with anything that comes along, or try to get someone else to fill the gap in your spirit. Eventually this missing part can lead to many kinds of sickness such as depression, autoimmune deficiency, post-traumatic stress, addictions and eating disorders, to name a few.

It all sounds quite grim... what hope is there for lost souls?

There is incredible hope. The great news is you can retrieve the missing part of you and become your whole, beautiful, creative, soul-full self.

Soul Retrieval

About a year after my hypnotic encounter with the 'child beast' I felt a burning need to rescue her. I had been doing a great deal of healing and coaching work with others, but it had come to a point where I couldn't progress any further. I was the wounded healer – I was the one who required healing. I needed to integrate this part of myself, and until I did, there would be no expansion with my life or my work.

One evening I came home after a particularly gruelling day at work, full of heartbreaking texts and holding-it-together attitudes. I headed straight for the wine bottle reflecting on yet another rubbish relationship that had hit the fan! I was boring myself with this repetitive story. I didn't know why the same old pattern had shown up yet again. There I was once more, dating an aloof, withdrawn, passive-aggressive type of male, who didn't know how to be intimate, and he had the audacity to say to me: "I think you want me to rescue you." Huh!

I pondered long and deep on these words. Why did they hit home so hard? There was definitely some truth behind my pain. I decided I needed to call back my creative power; 'I' needed to rescue me, 'I' needed to go and find the 'wild child beast', look at her, accept her, tend to her needs and embrace all she had to offer me.

The next day, I prepared myself for my first soul retrieval. I called spirit in for guidance, set the intent for a soul retrieval and slipped quickly into a trance-like state. Soon I entered my 'safe space', and a tree beckoned to me. It was the tree of trust that I planted a few years back in a journey. I flew over to it and found the trap door hidden in the trunk. Down, down, down, I went until I found myself crawling through earthy, dark, claustrophobic tunnels. They were shrinking and I felt as though I couldn't breathe.

Eventually, I came to a clearing where the air was fresh. I climbed down into a cave; here were many sad and lonely children all piled on top of each other. My child was alone. She had an arm hanging out as she lay splayed out and trapped under some rocks. As I moved closer to her, she was no longer the pale evil beast I remembered – she was fragile. I hurriedly pulled the rocks from her body and she looked at me with eyes of hope; she was a sweet, sweet thing; she was the daughter I never had and she needed me so desperately to pick her up and rescue her. I threw her over my shoulder and we flew back to a beautiful garden on a white winged horse that had appeared. As I washed her in the wishing well waters, her colour came back. I gently detangled her long, red hair and she became a flaming renaissance masterpiece.

Soul Loss Is Soul Learning

Since then times have changed. I retrieved three parts – a four-year-old, an eight-year-old and a thirteen-year-old. Each of them has returned with the gifts that I was seeking elsewhere. My soul retrievals have given me a sense of personal and creative power, which has paved the way for me to support others. Nowadays, I facilitate a large amount of soul retrievals with clients who have lost parts that are ready to return; feeling desperate to unlock their pain, restore their vital essence, and call back their creative power.

The effects of having a soul retrieval vary from person to person, although many of my clients do report feeling similar characteristics, such as a sense of relief, more playfulness, more compassion, lighter, more joyful, and strong and grounded in their body.

After a soul retrieval, it's important to integrate the soul essence into your emotional and physical body; it is part of your sun – the light you create from. Sometimes people only notice subtle differences until they do further integration work such as dialoguing with their lost soul part using techniques like the non-dominant hand exercise above, giving voice to and writing the story of their trauma, or by drawing on the support of their community – a counsellor, shamanic practitioner or friend.

When the integration is complete, the inner world and outer world become congruent, the soul is unmasked and able to unfold its pattern, and we are able to follow its direction; we can express our creative spirit, feel deeply, and take pleasure in life.

Soul Retrieval Journey

If you feel comfortable to do so, you can do a soul retrieval for yourself by following the steps below, or you can work with a Shamanic Practitioner like myself to do it for you. If you are not used to doing shamanic journeying, or feel unsafe or are unsure if you want to do it alone, I would advise you seek support from a professional.

Step 1:
Prepare your space and ensure you won't be disturbed. Play some shamanic journey drumming music to help you enter an altered and receptive state. (This can be downloaded from my website.)

Step 2:
Create a sacred space. Lie down on your back and get comfortable; you might want to use a blanket to keep you warm. Take a few deep breaths and set your intent clearly: "I am journeying to retrieve my lost soul part." Imagine that part in your mind's eye. Ask for support, call in spirit or your co-creator, god, the universe to guide you.

Step 3:
Start your journey by imagining yourself going down towards a safe, beautiful space, allowing it to unfold in your imagination. Don't worry if it feels like you are 'imagining', just go with it. Spend some time here to become acquainted with your surroundings. Next, look for a way to go lower or deeper – a place will open up for you. You may find power animals or spirit guides turn up to show you the way or accompany you.

When you find your child or lost part, ask them if they are willing to come back with you, ask them what they need from you in order to return with you. If they are happy to come back, bring them to your safe place and find some water to wash them in, nurture them and give them what they need. Integrate them physically into your body by blowing your child part into your heart three times. Sometimes the lost part can be angry or unwilling to come back with you – a bit like my first encounter with the 'wild child beast'. If this is the case, do not force it. Tell it that you love it and that you won't give up on it. You will come back when it is ready to come back.

Step 4:

When your journey has ended, give your thanks. Take the time to integrate 'your light' into your emotional and physical body. You can visualise your sun spreading through your entire body and use the previous non-dominant hand exercise and dialogue with them, dance with them, write their story, paint them, create an altar to honour them. And do something you haven't done for years and loved to do as a child, such as horse-riding or cartwheels.

Chapter 9

The Living Bridge of Story

Let's paint a picture....

The Great Story

She opened her mouth and swallowed it whole. What have I done she thought, as the sweet nectar of story slipped deliciously around her soul. Suddenly, her vision started to stretch in the most peculiar way – rather like a rubber band – and for one solitary moment she felt limitless. She put one foot in front of the other, feeling the crunch beneath her feet; it was the sound of old bones reshaping themselves into the path of wholeness and they gestured for her to follow them.

Suddenly, her world opened up with an almighty bang! Or rather, I should say worlds.

An entire universe was presented before her as, all at once, each story flung its doors wide open. The whispering invitations grew louder...

"Step inside and listen," they said.

She hesitated. Which story should she listen to? But this choice was soon taken out of her hands; her whole body began vibrating and she started to fall into hundreds and thousands of colourful stories. It was a mouth-watering experience.

As momentum gathered, she soared past countless tales – blushing romance, exhilarating thriller, rip-roaring comedy, finally tumbling across the grasp of death as she whirled into tragedy.

Faster and faster she travelled, hurtling at full speed towards the legend beyond death. She started to panic. "Help," she yelled, believing she would never go home again. A White Winged Myth happened to be flying by, and heard her plea. Just in the nick of time it swooped down to save her.

"Do not be alarmed," it said. "You are the heroine and this is your journey. All you need to do is drink this elixir and you will rise up exalted. There is no other way."

The golden elixir popped and bubbled; tempting the girl with mystery and adventure. She took a mighty gulp of courage and swallowed the potion. And as if by magic, started to rise up and transform into her Story of Greatness.

The stories we tell possess all we need to heal ourselves if we dare to look within.

Do you dare to discover your Story of Greatness?

The Heart of Story

Tell me the facts and I'll learn.
Tell me the truth and I'll believe.
But tell me a story and it will live in my heart forever.
Native American Proverb

What Does the Living Bridge of Story Offer the Life Artist?

On this living bridge, the magical force of story is inherent in every step. Be prepared to shape-shift rapidly, as you feel your way through this enchanting terrain. Do tread vigilantly; the appearance of each root tale can be deceptive; like quicksand they can suck you into a bottomless pit and hold you captive. Denial, struggle and resistance will smother you. The only way out of a stuck story is to care for it, relax into it, and surrender with arms open wide. Your motionless body will float to the top, and the story will respond by nourishing you; it will open the doors of your perception, quench your thirst with sacred medicine, and transform into a living illustration to escort you safely on your journey.

The Power of Story

Stories locate the heart in life. The power of the story is nothing new; after all, time began with a story. History was written with the winning story. You and I are hot-wired for stories; they bring value to our lives and help us to make sense of our experience. The foundations of our lives are built from these stories; we gain a sense of personality and identity through narrative and we craft belonging with our lovers, family, friends and children through storytelling. When you delve into the heart of your stories you tap into a vital source of your power.

We inherit stories, buy stories and create stories. But the bare bones of each story are simple. Just like our lives, a story has a setting, a series of unfolding events, and it has characters – with usually one central character that the events revolve around. By exploring your stories, you can travel to the heart of them and learn to care for yourself – you can 'feel into' your tales to see, understand and believe in 'all that you are'.

How Do We Bring Our Stories To Life?

To bring the spirit of any story to life we must invest in it with our emotion and belief and flesh it out with our perception – we become storytellers, 'storyhoarders' and 'storylovers'. Stories act as a rehearsal process for how we handle experience. They activate each part of the brain needed to experience a particular part of a story. For instance, have you ever wondered why you physically feel so scared when you read or watch a horror story? What makes it feel so real? Well, when you experience horror – even fictional – your brilliant brain turns on the ancient amygdala, which is the part of the brain associated with learning fear and terror. This rehearsal technique is helpful to us because we can have a go and see how the experience feels, before trying it out for real. Our understanding is developed so that we can store away different responses and ways of overcoming the werewolf that threatens to rip our throat out, if we should stumble across him one day.

It's the Way You Tell 'Em!

There are many reasons why we tell our tales the way we do; our culture, history, and sense of belonging are all embedded in our stories. Our problems start to arise when we are too busy trying to fit the stories of society – history, parents, children, and work – and we forget to tell our own unique tale.

You are a natural born storyteller, a creator of tales, and the 'way' you portray your life events shapes your identity and experience. You believe these stories to be true and adapt your future decisions accordingly. The edited versions that you tell yourself become your truth and – good or bad – your stories become fixed.

We've all had and been one of 'those' friends who goes on and on… We want to feel compassion for her, but we've heard the same story a million times already and, quite frankly, it's boring!

When we habitually tell sad, rigid and repetitive stories – and believe them – we become them. Our bodies adopt the fitting mask and posture, as well as the appropriate aches, pains and behaviours. Our minds think for the starring character, and our lives become theirs. This is how we smother and conceal our true nature.

With this information freshly at hand, it's a great time to ask yourself the following questions:

- What stories do I need to stop telling?
- What stories do I need to keep telling?
- What stories do I need to start telling?

Like most of us, your life story is often charged with a range of 'fixed' emotional experiences that still resonate for you, keeping your past stories energetically alive and running in the background. These 'fixed' emotional experiences shape your perceptions and inform your choices and daily habits. They influence who you become attracted to and what you choose to avoid. This is powerful stuff.

What Can We Do To 'Unfix' Our Stories?

Stories only limit us if they are fixed in place. If you want to change aspects of your life, create new dreams and tell a new story, you first have to find a new way of looking at the old. By telling your tale in a new way, you unfix it. You release the emotional charge it holds and lay its old bones to rest.

The telling is when you can spot the story working its magic. It becomes a mirror, a teacher, a friend, a guiding light revealing what you can now safely let go. You can see how your story has influenced your health, relationships, job, and attitudes; you can edit them and release what you no longer need. This liberates you to follow the guidance of your soul and tell your unique Story of Greatness – unrestricted, wild and free.

When you claim your power, and unlock the wisdom held in your stories, you can:

- Relate to and see universal truths
- Connect to and collaborate with others
- Free yourself from limiting patterns and restricting masks
- Love and care for yourself
- Discover and share your authentic truth
- Use your power to create a beautiful life

Let's get started...

The Story of Mind

How Many Stories Are You Telling?

As I am typing this I can hear the booming voice of a builder repeating a story as Shania Twain is singing on the radio: "Man, I feel like a woman, ahh, ahh, ohh." He is not conscious of it, but he is repeating a story. Now, it may be harmless for him, and it brightened my day as I imagined him unravelling his stockings on the scaffolding, but the lack of awareness about the stories we are telling and the power of the story can be a treacherous combination.

Our daily conversations function as stories and most of the time we pay very little attention to their nature and power. We are literally drowning in stories. There's the one about the car breaking down on your way to work, the boss who never listens, what your sister posted on Facebook, your runaway cat, what your best friend heard about you, the faulty scales, the man that never calls, what I'll do at the weekend, not to mention, the ongoing I can't afford it, what shall I wear or who will do the washing up saga!

How many stories do you star in each day? Have you tried counting them?

It's extremely draining, and even more exhausting shaking off the stories we don't want to be involved in, not to mention the internal ones we tell ourselves.

What can we do? We can become consciously aware of the stories we tell and the power they hold.

What Type of Stories Are You Telling?

I have witnessed prisoners escape, observed children go to Mars and seen illness dissolve, all through the power of the story. I have also experienced toxic stories, stories that cause illness, rip apart families and cause us to play small. The difference with these stories is that their toxicity lies in their un-telling, their secrecy; when they are told to another, a creative healing force comes into play.

How Many Stories Are You Wearing?

We know that we create stories from our experience. Something happens to us and our brains must make meaning from it by creating a story around the happening.

For example: Bill has left me because... I dyed my hair pink.

I sob for days and in my emotional state I believe this story and it impacts on my actions – I very quickly dye my hair back to the original brown colour.

A few months later I meet Fun Fred, all is going well and I feel like a change, I want to express my 'fun side' and decide to dye my hair purple. A few weeks later, Fred leaves me for Susan. This reinforces the story that if I dye my hair my boyfriends leave me. It reminds my brain of the first story, the tragic story of Bill. Bill and Fred become a force to be reckoned with and I vow never to dye my hair again. So, I become the brown-haired girl who can never dye her hair. I become my story.

There may also be hundreds of underlying stories glued to the Bill/Fred saga. Perhaps I can only look beautiful with brown hair, or dressed in brown clothes. And so, it goes on – layer after layer of story is created and woven into place. By the time we've hit 40, we are wearing a magnificent coat of tales.

What can we do about this? We can disentangle our stories – take a good look at the tales we wear and shed the ones that no longer serve us. Andy Warhol once said, "If there's ever a problem, I film it and it's no longer a problem. It's a film." This is one of the best ways of dealing with your toxic stories. Tell them; turn them into art and transform their energetic hold over you.

In the following exercise, you are invited to dig deep and uncover the layers of story that you wear. You will create your unique Coat of Tales.

The Coat of Tales

The following Coat of Tales exercise will help you to see what stories you are wearing and empower you to take them off whenever you please.

Resources required: scissors, a variety of cloth, needle, thread, pen, paper, paints, glue, staples, safety pins.

1. First, make a linear timeline of all the significant events in your life. Maybe five or ten year increments depending on your age. Include health, relationships, spirituality, work, and your service to others.
2. Using the timeline you have created, make a collection of all the emotional events in your life. These are events that when you think of them create a feeling or stir emotion within your body.
3. Now you're ready to create your Coat of Tales. Your coat is unique to you. It will encompass all of the stories you wear. Use image, word, pattern, collage, symbol, design, rhythm, repetition and any other ideas you have to represent each story and create your unique Coat of Tales.

   Grab an old sheet or some fabric as the base of your coat and attach your stories to it using glue, staples or safety pins or any other way that takes your fancy to make your coat.
4. When you have finished, explore the positioning of the stories; how you have chosen to connect them to the fabric. Look for any patterns that arise:

- What stories form the architecture and foundation of your coat?
- What are the repeated stories?
- Which ones are inherited stories?

- What attitudes surround your stories?
- How do they express themselves?
- What stories are hanging around that do not serve you anymore?
- Which ones are the untold stories?
- What is the great story keeping you alive?
- Which ones are the unfulfilled stories?
- What stories do you love?
- What stories scare you?
- What images reappear in your stories?
- Is there space for new stories?

5. Once you have explored the architecture of your coat, it's very important to wear it like a coat or cloak. Take your time...

   Become aware of sensations and feelings in the physical body as well as emotionally.

   How does it make you feel when you put it on?

   Are there any particular stories you don't want to be seen wearing?

   How does it feel to be able to remove the coat at any time?

   What lies beneath the coat?

   How does it feel when you remove it?

Are you naked when you remove the Coat of Tales?

As you can see, we have a very intimate relationship with our stories – after all, we end up living the stories we tell. Sometimes we disguise them, reinvent them, guard them and forget them, especially if we are held captive by a limiting story or repeatedly relive painful ones. When we reach this place it's time to both tell a new story and listen to the wisdom of the old.

The Story of Body

The Untold Tale

"Hush... don't tell."

The power held in these words alone is enough to send thrilling chills up your spine. But why?

Untold tales tend to lurk at the bottom of our psyche and take root in the body. They are given immense power through their secrecy and un-telling. These are stories that need to be heard by you. With your telling you can tap into their teachings; they contain insight, wisdom and answers to the questions you seek. When you embrace them, they can release you from energetic bindings, liberating your vital essence and empowering you deep in your core.

Sometimes we believe we have heard all the stories we are living, but many of us have an untold story that must be heard. This tale can literally halt us from growing in life; it needs to be expressed and honoured. Once it's told, you will find treasure in every morsel.

One of the best ways I've found of honouring and telling my untold tale is to hand it over to the realm of fairytale. The fairytale has a nurturing magic all of its own. It will hold your untold tale tight enough to safely reveal the energetic themes and patterns underlying it. The fairytale invites you to understand the fabric of your life choices, behaviours and beliefs and share your stories of loss, hope, and love.

Are You Living the Fairytale?

I'm sitting eating my breakfast from an old cooking pot. I'm surrounded by horses, twittering birds and there are even squirrels running over the old table. Every time I sit here I think of Snow White... This is the stuff fairytales are made from and a perfect place for me to write this section of the book.

I've taken myself to Rajasthan, the land of peacocks, palaces, and the fairytale city of Udaipur. The looking glass of India is dazzling me with her inspiration and magic; I've seen crystal four-poster beds, jewelled paintings, and I'm in the land of the Gods where anything is possible.

I hasten to add that this is definitely not a Disney-style life I'm leading. There's a huge dose of the nightmarish Grimms tucked away in my woods, which I will share with you in a moment.

The archetypal energies contained in a fairytale are highly influential and form a template for many of our life dreams. It's a story that runs in the background of our lives and shapes it. There is tremendous power in the fairytale; after all, it unconsciously shaped my life choices.

I was meant to marry Prince Charming and live happily ever after. Waiting to be rescued, I was one of those unconscious characters who had to climb into her own hair, take a good look, and dig deep into her roots to unearth her treasure. The fairytale helped me to do that in more ways than one.

I discovered that I was under a spell; an illusion that I 'should' be living a particular type of lifestyle and when that 'fairytale' didn't work out, life's shattered dreams opened the door to my soul's story – a Story of Greatness. It took me on a journey of transcendence, transformation and wonder. Just like the protagonists in the tales, I transformed 'my' disturbing events into personal and spiritual growth. You, too, can use the fairytale to unearth your treasure.

Why the Fairytale?

We grew up snacking on these ancient and wise tales. The fairytale is a wizened woman; a natural teacher, healer and visionary, and its form offers you total freedom; it provides your imagination with limitless scope. Symbolism, magic and metaphor ooze from its structural bones. Time and space can effortlessly move at any pace and you can speak uncomfortable truths without exposing yourself literally. This inbuilt safety mechanism is perfect for the spiritual, psychological and personal content you're enquiring into, wrapping them neatly in universal experience. Full of stereotypes and symbol, it's ripe for play and subversion.

Medicine Tales

Writing your untold story in the fairytale form waves a magic wand and provides you with a Medicine Tale. These stories care, heal and draw upon ancient wisdom. They become your art and, literally, take on a life of their own. As you drink their medicine they will shift shape and significance for you, nurturing your unconscious needs by creating hope and a path to wholeness.

When I wrote my untold tales using the fairytale form, I found that they provided me with indispensable medicine. They are the stories that the girl reads at the very beginning of this book, which brought her great truth, united her with the stars, and helped her to see her beauty. I have included these Tales of the Unexpected at the end of this chapter for you to read and use as examples.

Whatever your story turns out to be, trust that you will be offered hidden blessings which will free you from the emotional bindings of your story. Try it. It's fun allowing the fairytale to unfold.

Have a go at the following exercise and write your untold tale.

It's Time to Tell Your Tale

You may or may not know what your Untold Tale is, or you may have a few that are bursting to be heard. Either is fine.

Prepare your space so you won't be disturbed and have a pen and paper ready.

1. Take a deep breath and bring yourself into the present moment. Set your intent to voice your untold tale. Jot down any ideas, guidance, images, symbols and impressions you receive – they will form the basis of your fairytale.

2. Next, allow your fairytale to take shape. Start to write and allow it to flow. Do not concern yourself with the quality of the story, or the spelling. Allow your stream of consciousness to flow. And remember to have fun with imagery and character, making it as fantastical as possible.

Use the simple starting point of "Once upon a time".

When you finish your Fairytale read it out loud to yourself and reflect upon it: How does it make you feel? What do the characters represent? What symbolism has arisen? What does it mean for you? What can you learn from it?

The Story of Soul

What Is Soul Story?

This is a big question! Somewhere in the cosmic space between the known and the unknown lies the answer. My untold tales gave rise to my Soul Story; they cleared my energy path so that I was able to express my 'inner knowing' and unfold 'who I really am'. Your Soul Story is an unknown tale that belongs to you; it lays embedded in your star-studded roots beckoning to be told, and when you answer its call, you instantly know it's your truth.

How Do You Know?

One way of explaining 'inner knowing' is through the Akashic records. The concept of the Akashic field originates from ancient wisdom traditions where it's said that everything that ever has been or will be is written and accessible – it's a metaphysical field that conserves and conveys information and acts like the memory of the universe, containing your past, present and future. This field of information explains why with my healing work I am able to journey for a client without ever meeting them, receive guidance, and retrieve accurate information about them that I couldn't possibly know, to support their healing.

The Akashic records can be used to access any information you wish; you can use them to receive wisdom, gain insight, and connect with your Soul's true purpose.

However, they are not predetermined – we influence them. The only way to tell your Soul's Story is to express your true nature. When you choose to express yourself wholeheartedly here on earth, your authentic essence can unfold to reveal your knowing; creating alignment between your inner and outer worlds.

You can do this by following your heart and remembering that you are in a constant state of becoming all that you are. The Akashic records aren't written in stone, they are written in energy, which is continuously moving and changing as you and the planet do.

The Vital Wholeness of Soul

Our souls are crucial to our existence. They help us to feel the heart of the earth. They hold a template, a beautiful way for our pattern to unfold. Some of my shamanic work has called me to do what's known as Psychopomp work – working with souls that have passed over. My job was to retrieve their missing soul parts for them so they could move on to where they are heading. Now, I don't know where they are heading, but they obviously require a 'whole' soul to get there, as do we all.

The vital energy of your soul forms part of the great mosaic – the cosmos – and has a part to play. With your 'whole' soul as director you end up starring in the most exquisite performance here on Earth and beyond.

Your Story of Greatness

What is the Great Story your soul wants you to tell?

This book offers you many paths to uncover your true nature and live your Great Story. Only you can walk them and discover it. Your soul is imprinted with the beautiful vision that you and your co-creator agreed upon. And your authentic self can hear and express that story – it's perfect for you – emotionally invest in it and believe in yourself. Step into your wild wisdom and lead the way with integrity and heart.

Here are some probing questions to guide you:

- How do you want to live in the world?
- What type of world do you want to live in?
- What legacy will you leave for your children, your

grandchildren?
- What type of ancestor do you want to be?

The Unknown Tale

Just as we can free ourselves from the energetic attachments of our old stories we can also create new energies for our unknown stories. Your dreams are unknown, unlived stories, waiting to be brought to life.

Step 1:

Firstly, set your intent to discover your Great Story. In a stream of consciousness flow, write your Story of Greatness. This is the unlimited, ultimate dream. Just let it flow through your body and write everything that comes down. It doesn't matter if it makes sense to you. This should take around 15 minutes or as long as you wish.

Step 2:

Next, read back over your Story of Greatness and edit out all that you feel that will never arise, or you don't really care for. Prioritise your dreams.

Step 3:

Explore what you have left. Now is the time for story art. Draw out all the exciting things which have arisen from your Story of Greatness that you would love to make happen.

Step 4:

Next, using either drawing, paint or collage, create an image for each of the things that you identified and that you have decided to keep. When you have finished each image, stick them onto a piece of paper and create *'a Vision of your dreams'* to honour your story and remind yourself of where you are heading.

Tales of the Unexpected

Untold Tale number 1

The Generational Footbinder

One dark night, not long ago, snow fell on a lane in the heart of Cornwall. The man walked backwards so as not to show his footprints.

A little girl, four years old, lay dreaming of a galloping herd of Palomino ponies, their hooves wildly dancing, the sound of their bucking rhythm echoing through the skies. Their swishing manes touched the stars, whilst their tails tipped the ancient crystal, enticing the Earth's knowledge. Some say this was how they got their golden colour, some say this was how the Earth's heart beat. The girl was mesmerised by their wild beauty, dashing free. She jumped on their backs, floating through time, singing with the stars and playing in their dust. Faster and faster she soared, effortlessly. Harmony reigned.

The girl's window overlooked the graveyard; she was without fear, fascinated by the sparkling quartz and golden moon pools creating light where there was alleged to be darkness. She thanked God for her dreams.

One night, much like any other, a tall man, an extraordinarily tall man, came into her bedroom; he walked on stilts. He wore a tailcoat jacket, his hair was feathery white, but his face could not be seen, no matter how hard one strained to look. The girl was unaware; she was free, flying with her horses, soaring effortlessly on their backs as she usually did, gathering ancient wisdom.

And then something happened that would change her forever. Slowly a hand with thick, sweaty fingers, huge fingers (perhaps they were giant's fingers) thrust into her dream and violently pulled her off the horse. Scared and clutching a star, she landed with a thud into the hands. They stole her breath away.

The next morning was a rather peculiar morning indeed. All was not as it seemed. On this day, the girl did not dance the footpath to the well, in her habitual manner. Her sturdy bucket sprang a leak. The bountiful bees made no honey. And, the chickens laid not one egg. She was glad to see the nightfall.

That evening when the girl went to bed, for the first time she feared the moonlight. The graveyard looked unwelcoming and hard and the sparkling quartz was dead stone.

The allure of soft bones was too much and he visited once more. Snow was piling up, echoing footprints, bringing the chill closer; her breath misted over. His long shadow and billowy hands reached for her delicate, dancing feet. She lay very, very, very still. There was a rustling sound.

The tall man reached into his jacket pocket and revealed a beautiful hummingbird. Its rhythmic birdsong fluttered her ears with the scent of honeysuckle. Her lips twisted with the pleasure of melody and she relaxed. Then, in a flash, the man snapped the neck of the singing bird, dripping its blood into a big white bowl. Her shivers numbed the deathly silence.

Next, he reached into a different pocket and pulled out some odd-smelling plants. They were crispy and potent. He crumbled them into the bowl and mixed the concoction with those giant fingers. He placed both her feet into the pungent solution for what seemed like forever. She could hear the birdsong, radiating warmth from the freshly squeezed blood. Then, his leathery, pumice-stone palms gently circled her soles with expert craftsmanship. One by one, each toe was meticulously massaged, groomed, and then trimmed. Her eyes widened as he reached into yet another pocket and pulled out a sharp instrument and lay it beside her.

He began the process of reshaping the young girl's feet. Both left and right were soft, pliable and very warm. He took her left foot and curled each toe downwards towards the sole as far as her bones would allow. He repeated this action a second time, leaving the big toe intact, this time compelling the act further than her bones would allow. She counted the snapping sounds in her head, a bit like counting sheep. He formed a new shape like a twisted fragrant fist and, finally, set about severing the arch of her foot. The girl watched the dancing shadows fade from the wall as she bit into her down-filled pillow. The white feathers did not hear her cry.

His large hand picked up the sharp instrument; he used it to trim the ten-foot long bandages, which had been patiently soaking in the song-filled solution, and began his true artistry, sculpting a flower. The girl's foot dripped with song on each binding. The ball bounced no longer as it was drawn tighter towards the heel. Tighter and tighter, closer and closer he sculpted, until finally tapering the end of her foot into a point. Her attention was drawn to the tickling wings of the butterflies, which had gathered tenderly upon her free foot. He secured his work with embellishing loops of golden thread, stitching tightly with masterful precision, finally adorning this tour de force with a blue silk embroidered slipper.

He reached for her right foot, grimacing at the butterflies. "This is it, it's just you and me now, child," his smug voice whispered. Love was severed forever. The colourful wings lay broken on the floor. The moon disappeared as the little girl fell into a dreamless sleep.

The sun rose, the birds hollered and Little Jane woke without a trace of memory of the night's happening. You see, she was a very clever girl and had two minds; whilst her breath was held, one of those minds, the one she knew, was erased. But today felt different somehow for Little Jane; she now had fear in her heart and a shuffle in her walk. Her feet made a clip-clop sound just like a pair of hooves. This special walk will take some mastering, she thought.

Little Jane made her way down the winding staircase as usual. The excruciating pain was beyond her. She was much slower this morning and her mother was shouting angrily: "Little Jane, little Jane, why are you so lazy? Hurry, child, there is much work to be done."

Little Jane tried to please her mother's call, but clumsily kept slipping on the carpet of rotting flesh beneath her. With each step, the putrefying scent grew stronger. She rested midway on the stairs and cried two huge jugs of tears. "What is wrong with me?" she wept.

Her mother now shouted even louder: "Little Jane, where are you? What a terrible stench, go and wash yourself right this minute. And stop your blubbering, child."

Eventually Little Jane hobbled into the kitchen where her mother was busy making breakfast as usual.

"Good morning," said Little Jane as she went to kiss her mother. The mother was so horrified at the sight of the child that she threw the breakfast plate into the air and it landed on Little Jane's hair. Her mother had turned into a dark beast, a monster. She took a broom and beat her daughter.

"Stay away from me, you wretch, you are cursed," screamed the distraught mother who ran as fast as she could into the bedroom and locked the door. Only an angel could awake her from her flowery bed now.

Little Jane had no idea that she was such a terrible sight to behold. She had completely erased her memory of the night's dreadful event. The Generational Footbinder was a cruel man and had inflicted a powerful curse upon little Jane, a curse that would ruin her life forever: anyone who gazed at her horrific feet would be struck by darkness and change into a beast.

Little Jane pleaded, but the mother hid herself in the bedroom and lay under the covers like a slab of granite and would not come out. There was nothing the girl could do. Helpless, she sobbed some more and this time cried three jugs of tears.

All this commotion could be heard from the barn and her father came running to see what was the matter, but when he arrived Little Jane was nowhere to be seen. There were only three jugs of tears, he counted them, "one, two, three," and saw the ghastly feet of Little Jane peeping from behind the third jug.

"Please don't look, Father," she begged, but it was too late…

"You have done this to your mother," he growled at Little Jane, callously. "You're cursed. You are no child of mine. There is nothing here for you anymore. I forbid you to step into this house again."

And he banished Little Jane into the dark forest.

Untold Tale number 2

The Orange Boots

Some years passed and Little Jane had now grown. One day she was taking rest under her favourite juniper tree when she was woken by an enchanting serenade. She hid in the shadows of the branches.

"I am here to rescue thee. Fear not, sweet Princess, your foot is sweet…"

There was a long pause, some rustling of paper and a neighing sound.

"You shall go to the ball. Bang! Pow! Your carriage awaits."

The high-pitched voice disturbed the berries and made the leaves flutter.

Charmed by these magical words, Little Jane sank into the grass and lapped up the sweet sounds. She listened.

"I will search high and low for the Princess that fits this perfect slipper. I will not give up. There can be only one and she will be my true love."

The girl's curiosity overwhelmed her; she had to see who was delivering this perfect poetry. Slowly she peeped around the tree trunk and cast her eyes upon the most amazing creature she had ever seen. It was a delight to behold. Its head was large, soft and fluffy, with ears like velvet. Half-man, half-ass, this ridiculous monstrosity had captured Little Jane's imagination with the words that dripped from his silvery tongue.

"Who's there?" he called.

She held her breath and became as still as a statue.

"I demand to know who's there? You will of course need to come out of the shadows to get the benefit of my true glory."

Little Jane said: "Hello."

"Come and show yourself, child. Do not be afraid; my splendour and beauty can only be a delight for your eyes as well as your ears."

She came forward, her adulation swiftly growing.

"Mr Top-Bottom at your service, Top of the Bottom and Bottom of the Top," he said proudly.

Mesmerised by this strange creature, Little Jane replied: "That was so wonderful, Mr Top-Bottom. What is it that you do? What is it that transforms you? You are as intoxicating as honey."

"Darling, darling! Have you never heard of me? I am a thespian of true measure, the greatest actor of all time, master of disguise, illusion and suspense. I entertain the masses and they fall at my feet pleading for more. It's in my veins, dear girl. I awoke one day and thought 'I am destined to play the Dane', and true as the fates would tell, here I stand."

He paused, puzzled. "Why have you not heard of me? I am well known around these parts."

Little Jane explained that she had been banished to the dark part of the wood; not many entered because there was no reason. Nothing grew. She had come to collect the berries for their sweet-tasting juice...

He wasn't listening.

"I came here to rehearse my lines. I have the opening night in a few days and I needed some peace to ensure I could give my best performance ever." He paused. "My throat is rather parched," he said looking at the freshly-squeezed juniper juice.

"Would you like some juice, Mr Top-Bottom?" asked Little

Jane.

"I thought you would never ask, child. Where are your manners?" He gave a hearty laugh that wheezed and spluttered just like a donkey.

"And, do call me Top; all my friends do so."

They sat and Mr Top-Bottom proceeded to tell Little Jane of his most interesting life. One day a very jealous fairy put a spell on him and changed him to half-ass half-man.

"He was a most notable coward, an infinite and endless liar, an hourly promise-breaker, the owner of not one good quality," said Top-Bottom resentfully.

And of course this backfired – as all spells do on promise-breaking cowards. Top-Bottom's life had only grown more marvellous because of it.

"A powerful fairy queen fell head over heels in love with me. She recognised my star quality immediately and opened the door to my acting career. I have never looked back. I am in demand. I am even playing the lead role of the Prince and understudying the Fairy Godmother. I could play all the parts if only they would let me," he boasted.

"Was that what I heard?" asked Little Jane. "You are very good, Mr Top. I have never heard anything so inspiring and wonderful."

"Of course, child. I have this effect everywhere I go. You heard me reciting lines from *Cinderella*; this is a classic, highbrow and worthy of my attention."

You certainly do have a high brow, thought Little Jane, looking at his meticulously plaited mane falling over his brow.

"I will deliver it like no other," he continued. "All the critics are waiting for my interpretation of the Prince. I am treading the boards with finesse on this one. This is a very complex role... I have been combining the emotional memory techniques of Stanislavski with Brechtian secrets. It will leave them demanding more. Oh, how my gift will transform their lives."

He sighed in self-awe.

Little Jane didn't understand a word he was waffling about, but nodded complacently. She was just happy to have some company for a change.

Mr Top-Bottom took a sip of the juice and looked at Little Jane as if startled to see her; he was not the most observant of fellows.

"Dear girl, what is that monstrosity on your feet?"

Little Jane looked down in shame.

"Mr Top, sir, please cover your eyes, for my feet are cursed."

He laughed indignantly. "Oh, my dear, you have delusions of grandeur. You? Powerful enough to curse me?"

He started to sing with amusement:

"Ooh, here we have a scary Jane,

She has a truly ugly mane,

A lady fierce as a lion,

The most dangerous thing.

She will make me wild and foul,

With just one glance and a growl."

He shook his head and grinned with huge teeth.

"I am so clever, I must write this down. This will make a great ballad for my songwriting debut."

Then he took pity on Little Jane. After all, she had recognised his splendour, she was just ill-informed.

"My dearest child you have inherited some unfortunate genes, that is all. Care not, my dear, Top-Bottom is at your service."

He twitched his ears and thought for a second.

"But of course you will have to do one thing for me in return. If I help you, you must rehearse throughout the moonlight with me. You will play Cinderella."

Getting rather carried away with himself, he continued: "Of course, most people would pay for that privilege. You are in luck! I haven't indulged my charity work this year. This is a wonderful publicity story. I can see it now, 'The day Top-Bottom helped a poor wretch dance.' A tragedy reversed, written by and starring Top-Bottom. Finally, I will get to shake hands with the Queen!"

Little Jane listened with awe, and felt the flutter of hope brush her lips. "Right, child, make haste," said Top-Bottom handing her a script. "You have a read of this and I will weave my magic."

He reached into his bag, pulled out a loom and started to weave. At the drop of a hat he had produced the most extraordinary pair of orange boots. He neatly fixed them until there was no trace of Little Jane's bindings.

"Bless thee, child, thou art translated," he exclaimed, bowing proudly. "A fair lady in the making. Now you must honour your promise, let us rehearse, obscenely and courageously."

The moon shone and the sun rose for many days.

One morning Little Jane went dutifully to the large oak tree to practise her dance. Top-Bottom had taught her well. She loved the feeling of her dancing feet and was excelling in her skill. Sometimes she danced so much she shook violently and all the shadows that she collected that day would fly away, making her feel lighter.

Whirling like a Dervish, she twisted her body faster and faster and then fell to the floor with a bang. As she opened her eyes she thought she had gone to heaven. There stood an angelic Prince. She rubbed her eyes… was this a dream?

The Prince was bewitched by her dance. He dropped to his knees, exclaiming: "Only a Princess could dance like this. I have found my destiny. Will you marry me?"

Little Jane thought he must be crazy to want to marry her and was a little wary at first. Secretly, she was worried he would find out about her curse. But the Prince promised to paint her dreams and convinced her of his true love. So Little Jane married the Prince and went to live in the castle.

Three moons later the Prince woke up in a bad mood and asked Little Jane to take her boots off.

"You know I can't take my boots off," she said nervously. "They are stuck on."

Little Jane was worried that he would also fall ill with her curse just like her mother did all those years ago.

"I don't believe in silly curses," said the Prince. "Besides, I'm an angel, nothing can harm me."

Little Jane refused once more. This time her Prince became very upset and said she couldn't truly love him, unless she did as he asked.

Little Jane hated to see the Prince so upset and agreed to remove her boots. As the left boot fell to the floor so did the Prince. The angelic Prince had fallen ill with the curse.

Little Jane didn't know what to do. The Prince started to cut himself with his trusty sword. She put her orange boots back on straight away and locked the Prince in the attic.

Many years passed, Little Jane grew sad and weary and her boots faded to a pale grey.

One day Little Jane took a trip to bluebell woods to pick flowers for the Prince. She was always trying new things to make him happy again.

Feeling a little thirsty she knelt down at the side of the lake to have a drink. The ugly ducklings swam to the other side. Hmm, strange she thought, they usually come to say hello.

As she looked into the water she saw a Witch looking back and let out a cry of fear.

"Have no fear, I am here to help you," said the Witch. "I know your great secret, that you have an unhappy Prince hidden in the depths of the castle, under lock and key."

The Witch smiled to herself.

"I have the answer, but if I help you, you will have to give your magic boots to me." Little Jane thought about this for a while. Well... the magic had faded anyway and this would help get her Prince back, but she could dance no more.

"But what shoes shall I wear instead?" asked Little Jane.

The Witch looked over at the blooming lotus.

"I will make you a pair of lotus shoes and you can walk in those," she said.

In desperation Little Jane agreed and gave the Witch her boots.

The Witch gave Little Jane a song to sing. She had a lovely voice and started to sing sweet melodies that made the forest dance. Just as she reached the highest note she found she could sing no more. This was strange as she could still hear the sound of her singing.

Flying above Little Jane was a nightingale as blue as the sea and as green as emeralds. It flew around in a majestic circle singing at the top of its voice. The beauty of the bird and the gentle song was sure to make the Prince better. Little Jane was happy.

The Witch warned that the magic bird would only work if it were kept caged. Little Jane hobbled home with a beautiful gold birdcage and the bird sang merrily.

The Prince instantly softened when he heard the song and his angelic self began to shine. Little Jane was mostly happy. She sometimes wished she could sing the song and dance the dance, but only sometimes.

One day she was particularly tired and she went to the room as usual to bring the Prince some food. He looked different today, he was sitting on the stool with his head cast in shadow.

The cage was open and the bird was nowhere to be seen.

"The bird is sad," he said, "I had to set it free. I love it so much, it's the only way for it to survive. It's not natural to keep a bird in a cage."

Little Jane was shocked and angry.

"The bird was making you well from the curse, now you have no protection from me and I have no song," she cried.

The Prince was shocked when Little Jane confessed her secret pact with the Witch.

"You must go now to find the bird and retrieve your song. It is not the natural thing for you to be song-less," he said.

They hugged and with the Prince's blessing Little Jane unlocked the door and set him free. Then she set off on a long journey to find her song.

Untold Tale number 3

The Dark Night of the Soul

Little Jane was so tired and weary. There were thousands of birds in the woods and all of them had a song. How was she going to find her nightingale?

The night grew dark and cold and her feet ached. She looked down at the lotus shoes and saw they had worn away. The delicate petals were shrivelling.

Little Jane's heart sank and she took shelter by a large oak. Its branches were bare and dry. It was cold. She was alone and scared. The birdsong silenced and stillness descended. The forest was empty. There was no sound, no food, nothing.

"How could this be?" she cried.

Even the oak was hollow. Nothing made any sense. Nothing had any meaning. Nothing was the same any more.

As Little Jane wandered deeper into the forest, there was frost on the ground and the expectancy of twilight chilled her bones. The grass crunched as she shivered. She wandered further and deeper. Now lost, she entered into a heavy world of dark cold.

Little Jane hurried past frozen emerald butterflies, and the sight brought fear to her breath. She found that she was extremely wobbly. She longed for the orange boots she was so used to; the old petals and lumpy bindings on her feet made her feel nauseous.

Cold, exhausted and hungry, she took some rest by a nearby tree. As soon as she sat down and released her weight, the tree tumbled. This was strange; it frightened and confused her. Trees were known for their strength. You can always rely on a tree to hold you. She moved to another and the same thing happened. Then another. Where was she? Slowly she pushed the trunk of a tall poplar and again it fell. It looked like a tree, but it was made of paper. There was no strength in it. She was in a forest of paper trees. They were so tall that the moon was kept from smiling and the darkness grew thicker. She could feel it on her skin. She didn't know what to do and tried to think hard.

A caterpillar crawled by, stuffing its face with a crying leaf. "Ummm that's satisfying," he said. "But now I am lost."

"You are lost?" enquired Little Jane.

"Yes, I have strayed from my home and now I am lost."

He started to climb the tree to rest his full tummy. Little Jane warned him of the danger.

"The trees are pretending. They have no strength – they are paper trees. Be careful or they will fall over," she said.

"No fear, I have a special glue that helps me stick to branches," he replied. "I weave it from silk."

He climbed up and pulled out a silk hammock, attaching it with the glue. "Now I am ready, it must be time."

"Time for what?" thought Little Jane, marvelling at his ingenious bed, and wishing she had one of those to rest in.

"Why don't you take those rags off of your feet and make a bed," said the caterpillar. "You can use my special glue."

"I can't," said Little Jane. "They are part of me. I don't know how to take them off. And please don't look at them. I am cursed and anyone who looks at them falls under a terrible affliction."

"Please yourself," said the caterpillar. "I don't believe in magic and curses."

Little Jane settled for pulling a tall tree over herself for shelter. It was as light as a leaf. But the leaf, like paper, was very thin and kept blowing in the bitter wind. She stayed very still trying to trap hot air beneath it for warmth. The evening was so cold, the kind of cold that kills with its chill. The kind of cold that torments, the kind that freezes time.

The night was frozen and Little Jane's hands started to change colour. Through her blue veins, purple blood seeped from the fingernails. She couldn't move. She couldn't breathe. Her feet were the only part that were warm. Perhaps she should do as the caterpillar said. She had never thought about removing the bindings before.

Little Jane sat up and reached down to her feet. She longed for the happy times she had enjoyed, dancing with the orange boots. Now here she was alone, cold and lost. She had no memory of the fateful night and the artful Footbinder's presence; she thought that she'd had the bindings for ever.

She looked for a way in. Where do the bindings start? She noticed one thread sticking out and pulled it with her bleeding nail. She didn't know which was causing pain, her nail or the binding. She pulled harder and the bindings began to unravel. There was no going back now, the cold was unforgiving and constant. Quite quickly they came apart and she saw her bare feet for the first time in her life. They looked quite pretty, like flowers, she thought.

She gently woke the caterpillar and asked to borrow the special glue. She began weaving a hammock to cocoon herself for the night and protect herself from the ground. For the earth could not be trusted at night. When it was finished she attached it with the magic glue, hooking it into the branch, just like the caterpillar had done. But as soon as she climbed in and lay to rest, the tree fell. And with it Little Jane was flung from the cocoon of bindings.

A strange low vibrating buzz overcame the forest scene. It came from the easterly wind.

"What shall I do now?" cried Little Jane. She lay shivering in torment, her eyes fixated on the caterpillar sleeping peacefully.

"It's not fair. What is wrong with me?" she exclaimed haughtily.

The caterpillar did not stir. The girl did not know what to do. Anger like the breath of a dragon rose through her veins, engorging each one. She raised her hand and punched the ground fiercely. The ground collapsed and she floated down. The circulating fall was endless. Just like the cold, the light disappeared and she hit the bottom with a loud thud. She was very heavy.

Where was she now? She began to cry and cry. In fact, she cried so much she almost drowned in her puddle of painful tears. Their numbing effect was welcome to her aching breath. She surrendered. The buzzing halted, an empty stench filled her lungs. After the sobbing receded she sat perfectly still. Nothing moved. The only thing she could feel certain of was the darkness that lay before her.

Epilogue: The Gateway to the Sacred

You Paint the Pictures

Now is the time to close this book and step into your Great Story. You paint the pictures, so what is life going to be like for you? What does your expression of beauty look like on the planet?

Hopefully you've begun to answer these questions as you've progressed through this book. I hope that after reading and exploring the exercises, you have begun to love your vision of yourself. I hope you have begun to recognise the beauty and significance of your true nature, feel your connections and experience a deeper sense of belonging.

Living as a Life Artist, you will discover many ways to co-create your life. You will intuitively sense what is useful in order for you to stay aligned with the Star-Studded Mosaic. As you become familiar with conscious co-creating and do this frequently, your power will grow and you will become a stronger presence in the world. With your presence, you can influence and change the things you care about – be the change you wish to see and make a difference.

Before we end, let me share two pieces of wild wisdom to help you along your way:

Balance Is the Key To Beauty

Beware of suffering for your Art. It's easy to slip into the tortured artist archetype when you are busy shining your sun. Working with creative energy is immensely stimulating and consuming – if you're not balanced, you can burn out.

Remind yourself that you are working with a two-way energy flow. Every time you send your creative breath out into the world, you also need to take a breath inwards.

Know your limitations; if you feel like you are suffering and have lost your flow, take regular moon-time – gaze at the stars, receive, rest and be gentle with yourself. Create the space to be still, go inward, reflect, listen to your needs and communicate with your co-creator.

The Importance of Loving Your Vision

I want to leave you with love. It takes courage to live a soul-centred, creative life – it's not effortless. It asks you to face uncomfortable challenges and trust the whole that is working through you, so that you can recognise and follow the path that opens to you. This requires you to keep loving yourself – truly, madly and deeply.

We often get confused with the idea of self-love. Many of us are reluctant to develop it because we see it as being arrogant, selfish or self-serving. Yet the importance of self-love is paramount in all you do and create – it will keep you balanced and aligned.

Nevertheless, as I have found, it is often the hardest love to learn. Just when I think I've got it sorted, life challenges me, my truth is reflected back, and I see more of me to learn to love. Self-love takes conscious awareness and a lifetime's practice. Relax into it and look at yourself with a compassionate gaze.

Your self-love grows from living in ways that do not betray your authentic truth. If you are not 'feeling the love', it can be an indicator that you need to change your path. If you're in doubt about the way you're living, listen to the direction of your soul and have the courage to follow it. This will keep you loving yourself and aligned with your purpose.

As you live out your Story of Greatness, you will attract loving relationships, rare opportunities, magical synchronicities and wise teachers to support you on your creative journey. But remember that only you can play your part. Take delight in each moment recreating and uncovering new exciting things about yourself. Observe your truth as it is reflected back to you, learn from it and use it to create a beautiful life for yourself and a beautiful world for us all.

Art never ceases to surprise and rarely turns out as expected. Enjoy unveiling the mystery that is your life. Love it and live it fully with play and pleasure. And be ready to risk it all to stay true to yourself.

Scribble Notes

Setting the Scene

Scribble note: To delve further into the insightful mind of Virginia Woolf read *Moments of Being*.

Becoming a Life Artist

Scribble note: A great place to delve into Quantum Physics and the Observer Effect is the website sciencedaily.com.

Scribble note: To find out more about Joel Pearson's study on "The Functional Impact of Mental Imagery on Conscious Perception" head to the PubMed Central website.

Scribble note: To discover more about how artists see, seek out the study by Stine Vogt et al: "Expertise in Pictorial Perception: Eye-Movement Patterns and Visual Memory in Artists and Laymen", sagepub.com.

Scribble note: To feast on the works of Rumi try the book *Open Secret: Versions of Rumi* translated by John Moyne and Coleman Barks.

Scribble note: To introduce yourself to the works of Picasso try *Picasso* (Taschen Basic Art Series) by Ingo F. Walther.

Scribble note: To discover more about the Spiritual in Art try Wassily Kandinsky's book *Concerning the Spiritual in Art*.

Scribble note: To hear the tale about Amaterasu the Sun Goddess read *Ama-Terasu The Sun Goddess: Early Japanese Literature* edited by Charles F. Horne.

Scribble note: For further reading on creativity and quantum physics pick up *Quantum Creativity: Think Quantum, Be Creative* by Amit Goswami.

Scribble note: To introduce yourself to Anais Nin read *Mirages: The Unexpurgated Diary of Anais Nin, 1939–1947*.

Nature As Master

Scribble note: To discover more about the Dutch Painter Rembrandt head to *The Rembrandt Documents* by Walter Strauss and Marjon van der Meulen.

Scribble note: To delve further into how wolf reintroduction affected the ecosystem of Yellowstone National Park I recommend you visit the website yellowstonepark.com.

Scribble note: Check out the book *Quality Circle Time in the Primary Classroom: your essential guide to enhancing self-esteem, self-discipline and positive relationships,* by Jenny Mosley.

Scribble note: For more on the Philosophy of Indra's Net read *Hua-Yen Buddhism: The Jewel Net of Indra* by Francis H. Cook.

Scribble note: Check out Dr George Land's TEDX Tucson talk *The Failure Of Success* for more insight into the history of human innovation and the importance of creativity.

Scribble note: To discover more about Shinrin-yoku Forest Therapy head to the website shinrin-yoku.org.

Scribble note: Head to the *Journal of Urban Design and Mental Health 2017* on the website urbandesignmentalhealth.com for further reading on how natural spaces affect our well-being.

Scribble note: Head to the earthinginstitute.net for further reading on how earthing impacts human physiology and health.

Energy As Quality

Scribble note: Check out Suzanne Simard's insightful work for more info on the Ecology of Forests and the Mother Tree.

Scribble note: Check out Dr David R. Hawkins' book *Power vs. Force: The Hidden Determinants of Human Behavior* for a comprehensive understanding of the Scale of Consciousness and its relationship to truth.

Scribble note: To delve deeply into the world of chakras I recommend you visit the comprehensive work of Anodea Judith – her book *Chakras: Wheels of Life* is one of my favourites.

Scribble note: To introduce yourself to Shamanism check out Christa Mackinnon's essential classic – *Shamanism: Awaken and Develop the Shamanic Force Within.*

Scribble note: Read up about the Habits of Nature and Morphogenic Fields, dive into the work of Rupert Sheldrake.

Scribble note: To delve into the world of Alan Watts read the book *Become What You Are: Expanded Edition.*

Beauty As Muse

Scribble note: Head to the website greekmythology.com for further reading on the Muses.

Scribble note: My 'singing muses' were influenced by Homer's epic poem *The Odyssey.*

Scribble note: Read *Aching for Beauty: Footbinding in China* by Ping Wang for a powerful account of what women had to endure.

Scribble note: Check out Naomi Wolf's ground-breaking book: *The Beauty Myth* for an in-depth exploration into the pressure women face to conform physically. Still as relevant today as when it was written.

Scribble note: Read Margaret Atwood's novella *The Penelopiad* where she cleverly gives voice to the feminine in her retelling of Homer's *The Odyssey.*

Scribble note: For further reading on the Male Gaze head to Laura Mulvey's 1975 essay, "Visual Pleasure and Narrative Cinema".

Scribble note: To further explore how we look at art pick up the classic book: *Ways of Seeing* by John Berger.

The Pilgrimage to the Living Root Bridges

Scribble note: Head to Maria Popova's fantastic *Brain Pickings* blog to read more about EE Cummings or try to get hold of a copy of *A Miscellany Revised* from the library.

The Living Bridge of Theatre

Scribble note: I have drawn on references from *As You Like It, A Midsummer Night's Dream* and *Hamlet*. Take a look at *The Complete Works of William Shakespeare* to discover more.

Scribble note: For more on presence head to Patsy Rodenburg's book *Presence: How to Use Positive Energy for Success in Every Situation.*

Scribble note: For an introduction to theatrical conventions pick up Diana Devlin's classic book *Mask and Scene.*

The Living Bridge of Pattern

Scribble note: A wonderful book to explore your breathing is *Science of Breath: A Practical Guide* by Swami Rama.

Scribble note: For an introduction into the work and concepts of Carl Jung try his book *Modern Man in Search of a Soul.*

Scribble note: To explore beauty, pattern and truth from a scientific perspective pick up *A Beautiful Question: Finding Nature's Deep Design* by Frank Wilczek.

The Living Bridge of Mask

Scribble note: To dip a toe into the work of Oscar Wilde read *The Happy Prince and Other Tales:* "Man is least himself when he talks in his own person. Give him a mask, and he will tell you the truth."

Scribble note: If you fancy learning to work with Masks try Trestle Theatre Co., *trestle.org.uk.*

Scribble note: To dive into the work of Lucia Capacchione read *The Power of Your Other Hand.*

Scribble note: To delve further into the power of Soul Retrieval head to *Soul Retrieval: Mending the Fragmented Self* by Sandra Ingerman.

The Living Bridge of Story

Scribble note: To delve further into the realm of fairytale I recommend *Spinning Straw into Gold: What Fairy Tales Reveal*

About the Transformations in a Woman's Life by Joan Gould.

Scribble note: *Why Fairy Tales Stick: The Evolution and Relevance of a Genre* by Jack Zipes.

Scribble note: To hear more about Andy Warhol read his book *Fame*.

Scribble note: For thought-provoking information on the Akashic Records pick up *Science and the Akashic Field: An Integral Theory of Everything* by Ervin Laszlo.

Acknowledgements

To the many people who have helped to bring *The Art of You* to life. My heartfelt gratitude and love go to Jackie Butler, editor, publicist and dear friend, who has been walking alongside me on this journey every step of the way. It was invaluable having your expert eye to read and edit my work. You were the calm and patient motivator that transported me to the finish line.

To Christa Mackinnon, my dear friend, colleague and soul sister. Thank you for your time, support and belief in me. You encouraged me to go beyond my limits, and I am eternally grateful. Your expertise, kindness, generosity, and wholehearted support has been instrumental in getting this book out there.

To Mano, my partner, soul lover and dream sharer. Thank you for patiently pushing the wheelbarrow as I plant the seeds. Your deep-rooted love and support nurtures my buds and inspires me to blossom.

A huge thank you to the fantastic publishing team at O-Books for believing in me and giving *The Art of You* an opportunity to rise and shine.

Thank you to Stephanie Ayres whose incredible illustrations and cover design captured the essence of the book and motivated me along the way.

To my lifelong friend and soul 'mate' Craig Chapman. Thank you for your endless love, support, generosity and enthusiasm for all I do. You are my rock – the dancing diamond that lights up my life.

I have been honoured to encounter both beautiful minds and open hearts in the many wise and inspiring teachers I've had over the years. I want to especially thank Peter Kaye, Dr Frances Babbage, Dr Debra Myhill, Hiralal Verma, Pauline Blight, Nicholas Evans, Ajay Shrivastava, Deepthi TK, Dr Padmanabhan and Christa Mackinnon for guiding my passion and sharing your expertise with me.

To my students, clients and the Walk Your Talk family, who have also become my teachers. Thank you. Without you, there would be no body of work to share. With special thanks to Craig Duncan for permitting me to share his story and Harriet Graham for casting her artful eye over my work.

To my family: Paul, Shirley, Mark, Kate, Maisie and Zachary, thank you for loving all of me just the way I am.

Finally, I want to thank everyone who has stepped onto the stage with me and played a poignant role in my life and work. There isn't space here to mention all of you, but I do hope you know who you are. I'm truly grateful for your love, song, friendship, inspiration and teachings.

Resources

If you'd like to receive additional resources or work with me in person visit The Art of You website at www.vanessajtucker. co.uk.

Or head straight to India on a retreat and join the Walk Your Talk family at www.walkyourtalkretreats.co.uk.

Join me at the Women Weaving Change community, a place for women walking the path of the Empowered Feminine. www. womenweavingchange.com.

If social media is more your thing, come and say hi and get daily inspiration at:

www.facebook.com/VanessajTucker

www.facebook.com/Walkyourtalkretreats

Or share your creative endeavours and join the Sun Sisters tribe: a place for creative women to rise and shine. Find us on Facebook groups.

Instagram:

@dancingmytalk

@/walkyourtalkretreats

BOOKS

O-BOOKS

SPIRITUALITY

O is a symbol of the world, of oneness and unity; this eye represents knowledge and insight. We publish titles on general spirituality and living a spiritual life. We aim to inform and help you on your own journey in this life.
If you have enjoyed this book, why not tell other readers by posting a review on your preferred book site?
Recent bestsellers from O-Books are:

Heart of Tantric Sex
Diana Richardson
Revealing Eastern secrets of deep love and intimacy to Western couples.
Paperback: 978-1-90381-637-0 ebook: 978-1-84694-637-0

Crystal Prescriptions
The A-Z guide to over 1,200 symptoms and their healing crystals
Judy Hall
The first in the popular series of six books, this handy little guide is packed as tight as a pill-bottle with crystal remedies for ailments.
Paperback: 978-1-90504-740-6 ebook: 978-1-84694-629-5

Take Me To Truth
Undoing the Ego
Nouk Sanchez, Tomas Vieira
The best-selling step-by-step book on shedding the Ego, using
the teachings of *A Course In Miracles*.
Paperback: 978-1-84694-050-7 ebook: 978-1-84694-654-7

The 7 Myths about Love...Actually!
The journey from your HEAD to the HEART of your SOUL
Mike George
Smashes all the myths about LOVE.
Paperback: 978-1-84694-288-4 ebook: 978-1-84694-682-0

The Holy Spirit's Interpretation of the New Testament
A Course in Understanding and Acceptance
Regina Dawn Akers
Following on from the strength of *A Course In Miracles*, NTI
teaches us how to experience the love and oneness of God.
Paperback: 978-1-84694-085-9 ebook: 978-1-78099-083-5

The Message of A Course In Miracles
A translation of the text in plain language
Elizabeth A. Cronkhite
A translation of *A Course in Miracles* into plain, everyday
language for anyone seeking inner peace. The companion
volume, *Practicing A Course In Miracles*, offers practical lessons
and mentoring.
Paperback: 978-1-84694-319-5 ebook: 978-1-84694-642-4

Rising in Love

My Wild and Crazy Ride to Here and Now, with Amma, the
Hugging Saint
Ram Das Batchelder
Rising in Love conveys an author's extraordinary journey of
spiritual awakening with the Guru, Amma.
Paperback: 978-1-78279-687-9 ebook: 978-1-78279-686-2

Thinker's Guide to God

Peter Vardy
An introduction to key issues in the philosophy of religion.
Paperback: 978-1-90381-622-6

Your Simple Path

Find happiness in every step
Ian Tucker
A guide to helping us reconnect with what is really important
in our lives.
Paperback: 978-1-78279-349-6 ebook: 978-1-78279-348-9

365 Days of Wisdom

Daily Messages To Inspire You Through The Year
Dadi Janki
Daily messages which cool the mind, warm the heart and guide
you along your journey.
Paperback: 978-1-84694-863-3 ebook: 978-1-84694-864-0

Body of Wisdom

Women's Spiritual Power and How it Serves
Hilary Hart
Bringing together the dreams and experiences of women across
the world with today's most visionary spiritual teachers.
Paperback: 978-1-78099-696-7 ebook: 978-1-78099-695-0

Dying to Be Free
From Enforced Secrecy to Near Death to True Transformation
Hannah Robinson
After an unexpected accident and near-death experience,
Hannah Robinson found herself radically transforming her life,
while a remarkable new insight altered her relationship with
her father, a practising Catholic priest.
Paperback: 978-1-78535-254-6 ebook: 978-1-78535-255-3

The Ecology of the Soul
A Manual of Peace, Power and Personal Growth for Real People
in the Real World
Aidan Walker
Balance your own inner Ecology of the Soul to regain your
natural state of peace, power and wellbeing.
Paperback: 978-1-78279-850-7 ebook: 978-1-78279-849-1

Not I, Not other than I
The Life and Teachings of Russel Williams
Steve Taylor, Russel Williams
The miraculous life and inspiring teachings of one of the
World's greatest living Sages.
Paperback: 978-1-78279-729-6 ebook: 978-1-78279-728-9

Readers of ebooks can buy or view any of these bestsellers by clicking on the live link in the title. Most titles are published in paperback and as an ebook. Paperbacks are available in traditional bookshops. Both print and ebook formats are available online.

Find more titles and sign up to our readers' newsletter at http://www.johnhuntpublishing.com/mind-body-spirit
Follow us on Facebook at https://www.facebook.com/OBooks/
and Twitter at https://twitter.com/obooks